LEARNING RESOURCES
CENTRE

Havering College
of Further and Higher Education

709.5

HL

6537188

128425

Buddhist *art*

Bodhisattva Maitreya wears a *pancha tathagata* crown in this image from the Thikse monastery.

Preceding pages 2-3: A section of Bhava chakra or Sansara chakra painted on the walls of the verandah of cave no. 17 at Ajanta, India. The cycle depicts five forms of life, the *pancha gati*. According to a *vinaya* text, Lord Buddha had asked Anathapindada to paint the wheel of existence in five divisions at the entrances of monastic complexes.

Facing page: A delicate sculpted deity, an iconic form of a bodhisattva.

Buddhist *art*
In Praise of the Divine

Dr Shashibala

Foreword by Dr Lokesh Chandra

Lustre Press
Roli Books

**Dedicated to my father who kindled the
spark of knowledge in me**

All rights are reserved. No part of this publication
may be transmitted or reproduced in any form or
by any means without prior permission from
the publisher.

ISBN: 81-7436-217-7

Text: Dr Shashibala
Foreword: Dr Lokesh Chandra

© **Roli & Janssen BV 2003**
Published in India by
Roli Books in arrangement
with Roli & Janssen BV
M-75 Greater Kailash-II (Market)
New Delhi 110 048, India.
Phone: 26442271, 26462782
Fax: 26467185
Email: roli@vsnl.com
Website: rolibooks.com

Printed and bound at Singapore

Contents

Foreword

Jambhala painted on a wooden cover of a sixteenth-century imperial manuscript from Tibet.

Preceding page 6:
Buddha in the *Dharma-chakra-pravartana-mudra* or the Turning of the Wheel of Law posture from Sarnath.

In Buddhism, art is the flowering of Being so that it can discover the great calm within, a dialectic of light and shadow, wherein colour and form rain substance. Scrolls, murals, icons, stupas, sancta and other manifestations are all Visual Dharma. They demand of us: 'Follow us to the spring and descend deeply within yourself.' They create a space for meditation, they awaken cosmicity within us, they are a wave to lead us to the progressive sea, to a track of expanding consciousness, or as is said in the stirring crescendo of the Heart Sutra of the *Prajna-paramita*: *gate gate paara-gate paara-sangate bodhi svaha.*

The Vinaya-sutra on monastic discipline narrates that Anathapindada constructed the nine-storey monastery of Jetavana. Before offering it, he asked Lord Buddha about the colours to be employed and the themes to be painted. While the painters worked, the monks washed near the murals, dirtying them. The monks' fire blackened the murals with smoke. The Buddha reprimanded them; and later the care of murals became a part of monastic discipline. When the paintings were completed, people came to look, admire them, and they became paths of entry into Dharma. Beauty was a way to beatitude.

A Buddhist treatise on art, the *Citra-laksana* of Nagnajit (available only in its Tibetan rendering), dilates on the natural metaphors of the eyes: 'The eyes of yogis, bespeaking equanimity, should be made to resemble a bow of bamboo. The eyes of women and lovers should resemble the belly of a fish. The eyes of ordinary persons should resemble a blue lotus. To express fright and crying, eyes resembling the petal of a red lotus should be used. The eyes of those troubled by anger and grief should be painted resembling a cowrie shell.' These metaphors derive from natural processes wherein the artist emulates the pulsations and creative rhythms of the universe. Art oscillates between the body that is a temple and the mind which has its full awakening. The instinctive and the intuitive create supreme order. Nagnajit says that a painter or a sculptor should have a perfect understanding of the proper proportions of the human or divine body. Proportion is essential for worship, as the images must be satisfying to our eyes. To paint is to evoke.

The icon is the body of the divine made real, the concrete shape of an invisible transcendent vision. The Unmanifest (*amurta*) concretises into a Manifest, a *murti* or image, to be seen with the eyes of faith. In the creative embrace of a sculptor or painter the subtle assumes plastic form which, in turn, transforms the visible world into transcendence. The interlacing of the body and limbs of a couple in embrace is the reunion of Person and Nature, of *Purusha* and *Prakriti*, in the passionless contortions of rapture, the cosmic creative process, the *yab-yum* of Tibetan iconography. The icons are a language for those in whom passion exists in the highest degree, beyond which they have to ferry to the Yonder. Intimacy and passion are transformed into blissful and enlightened states of awareness.

From the understanding of the Many emerges the triumvirate of gods, goddesses, and ferocious beings known as Krodhas, Vidyadharas, and Dharmapalas in Buddhist parlance. The three constitute a central part of our cultural consciousness. They find valid space in Vajrayana art and thought and have to be transfigured: anger has to be crossed over by non-anger and violence by non-violence to reach the still centre of the Sublime. One has to draw out the Dharma that is within oneself. The body contains the entire universe (*dehe vishvasya maananam*). In the higher stages of meditation, the body and cosmos are assimilated, the Dharmadhatu is shining light and concentration is its perception. By mystic light (Tibetan: *hodgsal*) one purifies the *samsaric* infections. The divine forms do not remain in distant heavens, but descend into us: I am the cosmos and the Buddhas are in me.

Dr Shashibala presents in this book a vivid survey of the rich morphology of the Buddhas and Bodhisattvas, gods, goddesses, and ferocious protectors, the architectonics of the stupa, and other sacred structures. It crystallises the grandeur of meditation and the heart of panhuman culture in the mysterious intrinsic necessity of the spirit. Dr Shashibala's enunciation is an endeavour to express the basic form and meaning in the vast spaces of Buddhism: from Buryatia and Tuva in the extreme north, to Central and East Asia in between, and down to the plains of India and Southeast Asia. She chronicles the immense panorama of the Visual Dharma across forbidding mountains, untamed rivers, waterless deserts, icy howling winds, silent spaces of the plains, in the plenitude of history and in the dynamism of life, to attain to the core of existence and transcendence, to what the heart desires and the mind seeks.

Dr Lokesh Chandra

Buddhas in different forms inside the Thikse Monastery in Ladakh, India.

Preceding page 7:
Garlands hang down from the mouth of the Kala Mukha, the face is topped by three jewels; such faces adorn temple entrances or pillar tops.

Shakyamuni Buddha sitting in a
cave in the valley of Lhasa. The
right hand is touching the earth
while the left is placed in the
lap and holds a bowl.

A MONK WITH THE DRAWING OF A
VISHVA-VAJRA. THE SYMBOL IS DRAWN
IN THE FRONT AND CONSISTS OF
TWO CROSSED THUNDERBOLTS. IT
REPRESENTS ABSOLUTE STABILITY.
A *VAJRA* IS THE SYMBOL OF
INDESTRUCTIBILITY, OF THE ESSENCE
OF ALL PHENOMENA; AT THE CENTRE
OF THE *VAJRA* IS THE AUSPICIOUS
SIGN OF THE SWASTIKA.

Introduction: The Beginnings

Siddhartha, the Prince was from Kapilavastu, from a *kshatriya* family. Gautama was his family name. His father King Shuddhodana tried hard to confine him to the luxurious atmosphere of the palace to restrain him from following the path of asceticism. But when Siddhartha saw the sufferings of the world, he was so disturbed by the common phenomena of human existence that he resolved to renounce the world. Quietly, he left the palace at night. Yashodhara, his wife, and Rahula, his son, were sleeping unawares. He went to a forest, cut off his princely hair, changed his royal clothes with those of a wanderer's, and set out in search of truth. He sat in meditation under the Bodhi Tree in Bodh Gaya, and finally attained Enlightenment after bearing constant hardships.

Now the Prince had turned into a *yogi*, he had gained *bodhi*. He became known as Gautama Buddha. He decided to preach to save humanity from suffering. The Buddha gave his first sermon at the Deer Park at Benaras. The Wheel of Law was set in motion. The Buddha's personality was so overwhelming that people began to throng in adoration to listen to him. Today, the Buddha's philosophy is contained in Sanskrit or Pali texts or in their translations in various languages of the Buddhist countries.

Though Buddhism was founded in the sixth century B.C., the earliest records can be traced only to the reign of Emperor Ashoka (273-232 B.C.) in the form of stone inscriptions that explain the word *Dhamma* as a system of duties and values. One of the inscriptions records the restoration of a stupa. Mention has also been made of the miraculous construction 84,000 *stupas* by Ashoka for the Buddha's remains. Stupas that contained the relics of the Buddha were worshipped as the Buddha himself. No monuments prior to the third century B.C. have been excavated so far.

The Buddha had denied image worship, so Buddhist art had its beginning with symbolic representations of the Enlightened One. The presence of the Buddha was indicated by an empty seat, his footprints, the Wheel of Law or a lion. But the Mahayanists demanded something substantial to adore him. Iconism gradually replaced aniconism. The Buddha was visualised with Bodhisattvas, disciples, followers, *arhats*, guardians, flying angles, *devas,* and demigods. The images of the Buddha were fashioned for the first time during the reign of a Kushana king, Kanishka. A schist statue in the Gandhara style made with the red stone of Mathura set forth the tradition.

Earliest Buddhist art emerged as a bridge between Vedic nature worship and the aniconic representation of the lord. A historical personality was endowed with divine

Vajradhara holding thunderbolts in his hands crossed near the chest.

13

attributes. The majority of later works are of Mahayanic inspiration. The Mahayana movement emerged in south India in the first century A.D. and was preceded by four councils held at Rajgriha, Vaishali, Patna, and Kashmir.

The Mauryans were patrons of early Buddhist works of art. Cream coloured stone columns of *chunar* sandstone erected by Emperor Ashoka are beautiful artistic expressions. Animals are sculpted on their tops and the wheels are in relief on the bell-shaped capitals.

The early account of the Buddha's birth and life are told and painted as *Jataka* stories. The philosophy contained in the *sutras* is visualised in wall and scroll paintings, in huge and varied pantheons, mandalas, and other formats. Buddhist art flourished in its Hinayana and Mahayana forms. A variety of Buddhas and Bodhisattvas were painted and sculpted over the centuries to aid suffering humanity and lead them to salvation or show them the way to paradise. These Buddhist art treasures are preserved in monasteries, museums, and private collections.

The teachings of Shakyamuni Buddha crossed the boundaries of India and reached most of the countries of Asia. The teachings became the mind-ground of the Asians, bringing about a spiritual, philosophical, and artistic unity among them. Monks carried the Buddha's vision in its Hinayana, Mahayana, and Vajrayana forms. Emperor Ashoka laid the foundation of giving state patronage to propagate the law. In the later centuries in various countries kings and emperors gave ample support for building monasteries, housing images, carving cave complexes, copying, translating, and distributing sutras.

Strengthened by royal support, Buddhism entered a phase of vigorous expansion. Its confines were opened up for the lay devotees. It took the Silk Route to enter China via Central Asia from Afghanistan and the northwestern frontiers of India. From there, it spread to Korea and Japan and via sea routes it travelled to the countries in the Southeast. From the Himalayan mountain ranges, it was disseminated to Nepal, Tibet, Mongolia, Siberia, and Manchuria. Their artistic creations are based on Lamaist forms. Artists from diverse cultural backgrounds created new styles, giving a rich and subtle palette of expression to Buddhist art.

Japanese monks perform the circumambulation of a stupa built near the Ashokan pillar at Vaishali. The pillar is topped by a lion; such pillars were erected by King Ashoka and Buddhist teachings were engraved on them.

Devotees circumambulating the stupa at Sarnath. Lord Buddha gave his first sermon at the Deer Park here to set the Wheel of Law in motion. Sarnath produced narrative sculptures of a high order, chiefly showing events from the Buddha's life.

15

A Nepalese stupa with a
thunderbolt, the *vajra*, a symbol of
supreme divine power. Power is
transvalued in Buddhism into great
compassion, itself the strongest
power in the universe. Different
animals decorate the dome of the
stupa to symbolise the supremacy of
the Buddha over all spheres of life.

PRECEDING PAGES 16-17:
Tibetan monks hold their masks
after a dance performance.

Architecture: Divine abodes

Stupas: For the Buddhas

Stupas were royal monuments. Their presence in a place was an assertion that, that was an integral part of the dominion. The tradition comes down from pre-Buddhist India when stupas were built for *chakravartins* or emperors. The Buddha demanded that the Awakened Ones be honoured in a similar manner. Soon stupas became important symbols as visible traces of Buddhism all over Asia. From massive monuments to tiny votive offerings, stupas have many levels of meaning. At the most profound level, they are symbols of *Dharmakaya*. Dharmakaya Buddha is beyond all forms, he is the essence of all beings. Depending on the nature of the stupas, they can be broadly classified into three categories: as reliquaries, they contain ashes of the Awakened Ones, as memorials, they mark important events in the life of the Buddha, and as votive stupas, they are symbols of meritorious acts.

These divine structures began to appear during the life of the historical divine. The first stupas were built by two traders, Trapusha and Bhallika, to venerate the refuge-giving three gems: the Buddha, the *Dharma,* and the *Sangha*. They requested the Buddha to give them a relic that they could worship, a relic that would signify the presence of the Buddha even in his absence. The Buddha conceded, cut off his nails and a tuft of his hair, which he gave to them and asked them to build stupas. He promised to provide stones for the stupas. Trapusha and Bhallika built stupas at Keshasthalin for the hair, at Valuksha for the nails, and at Shiluksha for the stones he provided. The forms of the stupas are not determined by rigid technical specifications, but are based on experiences and intuitions that differ from place to place. Stupas could either be dome-shaped, built in the form of a tower or be pyramidal. There may be *shatadwara* stupas that have either many doors or caves, while *prasada* stupas and five-element stupas (also known as *gorinto* in various architectural traditions) developed symmetrically around a central point.

Dome-shaped stupas have a hemisphere as their most prominent feature, with a small central chamber in which the relics of the Buddha are kept in a casket. Their core was made of unburnt bricks,

BEGINNING OF ICONOGRAPHIC
REPRESENTATION OF THE
BUDDHISM

while the outer surface was made of burnt bricks covered with thick plaster. Some stupas are magnified versions of the existing smaller ones. The prototypic form is seen primarily in India, Sri Lanka, Burma, and Thailand.

In India the form can be traced back to Sanchi, Bharhut, and Amaravati. Stupas on the Indo-Nepalese border (*ca.* 400 B.C.) are presumed to be the earliest known ones. The most beautiful one at Sanchi (*ca.* 250 B.C.) is roughly contemporary to the one at Bharhut.

Bharhut was known for its monuments that were built during the Shunga reign in the second century B.C. It was razed; nothing survives but the shallow circular depression around a slightly raised circular ground, and parts of the railing and posts. The railing was carved luxuriantly. The bas relief are an important source of the art traditions, beliefs, and practices of the times. Medallions on the posts and crossbars in Bharhut are replete with motifs like buildings, animals, lotuses, floral compositions, flowering plants, the *dharmachakra*, Maya's dream . . .

The *Chaitya* Hall at Bhaja (first century B.C.) is the focal point of the cave, a symbol of the Buddha and his teachings. A high-vaulted ceiling, a central nave, two side aisles, an arched roof, and an ambulatory are the main characteristics of the hall. The façade is carved to simulate a wooden construction; long railings and grilled windows are carved around the hall. The sculptured *yaksi*s are extraordinarily sensuous.

At Anuradhapur in Sri Lanka and the Yun-kang caves in China, the stupas are placed on elephant backs indicating the royal nature of the stupa. This shows the telescoping of the Buddha as the world monarch.

Reliquary stupas were first constructed when the Buddha entered *parinirvana*. His remains were eventually divided into ten parts, of which eight were given to kings to erect stupas. The ninth part—the vessel that contained the ashes—was destined for the Brahmin Drona who built a stupa over it. The villagers living close to the site of the Buddha's cremation erected a stupa over the tenth part—the embers of the crematory fire.

When Emperor Ashoka embraced Buddhism and pledged to propagate it, he recovered all the relics and sent them to 84,000 sacred places all over India and abroad to be enshrined in stupas. Each object used by the Buddha, including his alms bowl,

Rows of small stupas cluster around the Svayambhunath stupa in Nepal.

facing page:

Eyes painted on the *harmika* rise to the summit of the dome of the Svayambhunath stupa in Nepal. They represent the eyes of the Buddha in meditation.

staff, and robes became sacred. Later, the ashes of Buddhist saints were also venerated as sacred deposits.

Memorial stupas do not contain relics. They were first built at sites marked by important events in the Buddha's life: Kapilavastu, the Buddha's birthplace; Bodhgaya, where he attained Enlightenment; Sarnath, where he delivered the first sermon; and Kushinagar where he entered the final rest. Later four more sites were added to the existing ones, giving rise to the concept of the 'eight stupas'. When eight stupas were built in Tibet, they came to symbolise the eight events in the life of Shakyamuni: his birth; renunciation; encounters with a beggar, a sick man, a corpse and an ascetic; meditation in the forest; assault by Mara, the demon; enlightenment under the Bodhi Tree; sermon at Sarnath; and the miracle at Shravasti or the *parinirvana*.

Some of the other sacred places were Sankissa, where the Buddha had descended from the Trayastrinsha heaven, Rajgriha where he had tamed the elephant Nalagiri, and Vaishali where he had been offered a bowl of honey by a monkey.

A votive stupa could be an offering to earn merits, or an act of sacrifice. One who donates a stupa is either a munificent being *(danapati)*, or a sacrificer *(hota)*. Several elements of each votive stupa merge into one organised whole.

The fence is the outermost part of a stupa that separates the sacred from the profane. It is decorated with auspicious signs to ward off

evils and to prepare the mind of the devotee for worship. Four gates open towards the four quarters of the world to invite all beings.

The dome or cupola is the most important constituent of a stupa. It is the mediator between a base and a crown. Its shape is compared to that of a water bubble, an egg, or a heap of grain *[dhanyarashi]*. The inside of a stupa is a symbol of latent creative power. Around the dome is a circular terrace called *medhi* for circumambulating along the course of the Sun.

The *harmika*, an altar-like structure that rises to the summit of the dome, symbolises a sanctuary enthroned above the world, beyond death and rebirth. In the earliest stupas, a *harmika* is crowned by an honorific umbrella made of stone. It is from here that the central axis emerges from within the edifice. In Nepal and Tibet, eyes are painted on the *harmika*. They represent the eyes of the Buddha in meditation.

The central axis was meant to express stability; often made of wood, it rises up to dominate the stupa in the form of a staff bearing parasols. The parasol is a regal symbol. It has been an emblem of kingship throughout Asia; it indicates the royal nature of the building it shelters. The Buddha is a monarch, the Wheel-Turning King whose Dharma rules the cosmos. Honorific umbrellas were used as an abstract imitation of shade-giving trees. When they increased in number, they were fixed one on top of the other, transforming the whole back into the shape of a tree. Rings also symbolise different stages of consciousness on the way to Enlightenment.

The spire, the pole that supports the finial of a stupa, sometimes penetrates deep into the body of the dome. At times it rises from a supporting stone set in a shallow cavity on the summit, and can be a wooden post or an iron pillar.

The pinnacle of a stupa is commonly capped by a vase or a jewel. A full vase is a symbol of the plenitude of an enlightened mind. The spire of the Tibetan stupa ends in a Sun and Moon finial representing *nada* and *bindu*, or the point of void. A flaming jewel represents the elemental ether.

Svayambhunath, the most venerated stupa in Nepal, was founded in A.D. 400. The original stupa lies hidden behind an elevation of a relatively recent date. Its dazzling gilt finial is protection against the summer rain.

Sri Lanka has preserved the original shape of the stupa. The Thuparama stupa, the earliest one, was built during the reign of Emperor Ashoka (272–32 B.C.). Instead of the Sanchi-like railings, it has an enclosure for circumambulation on a raised ground. The stupas at Anuradhapura and Polonnaruva are prototypes of the ones at Sanchi and Bharhut.

Burmese stupas can be bell-shaped like the Sri Lankan stupas, or they are in the form of reliquary caskets. They often comprise a splayed bell. Parasols are piled up on spires to adorn them. A triple wrought iron umbrella was added by the Burmese to the summit.

Chedis in a variety of styles are a major attraction at Wat Phra Keo, known as the Temple of the Emerald Buddha, in Bangkok. Phra Pathom Chedi at Nakhom Pathom is 393 feet high. Originally, it was founded by the Dvaravati Mons in the fifth century. Later it was converted for Brahminical use by the Khmers. King Monkut rebuilt it in 1860, and King Chulalankorn embellished it with beautiful Chinese ceramic tiles.

The greatest of all the stupas or stupa complexes in Burma is the Shwedegon Pagoda built by King Aniruddha and his son Kyanzittha. The Shwedegon Pagoda stands on three, very high, square, stepped terraces adorned with glazed terracotta panels. The bas-relief on the panels recount events from the Buddha's former life. Effigies of Naths around the pagoda render homage to the Buddha.

Nepalese stupas are often found in towns, mostly in *vihara* settings. Carved relief on the base of domes form an important part of the decorations. By choice, the stupas are erected above water sources. Swayambhunath is conceived as the primordial Adibuddha. It is most venerated as a temple of the *vajrayana* school. It is also viewed as a sacred reliquary enclosing the perpetual flame, jewels, and corporeal relics of the Buddha, the Bodhisattvas, and the pious ones. Its gilt finial dazzles in sunlight. Bodhnath Stupa, the largest in Nepal, is believed to be a reliquary of the mortal remains of the Kashyapa Buddha, the predecessor of Shakyamuni. Hundred and eight niches are carved on its base.

Terraced or Meru Stupas: Terraced stupas stand on the summit of Mount Meru. Their domes are smaller in size, and erected on stepped pyramid-like bases. Such stupas are found mainly in Burma, Cambodia, Thailand, and Indonesia. The finest one is Borobudur in Indonesia. It represents a stupa pavilion at the summit of the cosmic mountain and is built on five square terraces. The walls enclosing the galleries are sculpted with a profusion of relief inspired by the main events in the Buddha's life. Scenes from hell are concealed in the basement. The three circular terraces are not enclosed. Seventy-two Buddhas sit in these pierced-domed stupas. This in-dwelling presence is sometimes depicted through images on the outside of stupas' domes. The same concept is reflected in the metal stupas of South India that open up to the world only to reveal the Buddha within.

Shatadwara or Prasada Stupas: Mountains and caves are two archetypes of sacred Buddhist architecture, relayed in the cave temple and the stupa. The two symbols often combine or overlap in architectural expressions. The stupa contains a hollow chamber like a cave, while a cave temple contains a stupa, as in Ajanta. The Ananda Temple in Burma is a cave with subsidiary caves radiating in many directions.

The Gyantse stupa in Tibet is called a *kumbum*. The *kumbum* constitutes a special category, being a specific monumental type with many auspicious doors, myriad icons, and gorgeous murals. Rooms or doors symbolise caves. The

An entrance gate and a section of the railings of the stupa at Bharhut, constructed by the Shungas on the crossroads connecting Uttara Koshala with Chedi and Dakshina Koshala. The stupa has been destroyed and the section is housed in the Indian Museum, Kolkata.

kumbum with its seventy-five chapels is the wonder of the Tibetan Buddhist world. It is built in the typical traditional Tibetan style. Hollow within the inner circumference, the stupa rises in the middle of a natural enclave. The Buddhist teachings in their simplest form are depicted on the lower storeys, while the secret and subtler teachings of the esoteric doctrine are depicted on the upper storeys. A pilgrim may go inside, meditate, climb up the stairs inside to reach the highest point of the stupa.

Gyantse represents the *Dharmakaya*. Almost the entire pantheon of Tibetan Buddhism has been depicted in it. Tantric cycles have been painted on the walls of the first three levels. Indian and Tibetan masters who spread Buddhism occupy the fourth level. The *harmika* comprises two storeys. Mandalas are painted on its walls. An octagonal chapel inside the spire crowns the building, and houses the gilded copper statue of Vajradhara, conceived as the Adibuddha.

Multi-storeyed Pagodas or Shikhara Stupas: Stupas are called pagodas in eastern countries. In Tamil it is known as *pagavadi*, a house that belongs to a deity. *Pagavadi* is derived from *bhagavati*, the feminine form of *bhagavat*, the adorable, the divine. Bhagah is the God of Wealth. There are numerous multi-storeyed pagodas in the Far East, made of bricks or wood. The layers are indicated by a series of relatively inconspicuous cornices, or by windows. A finial stands on the summit of the stupa.

The Sino-Japanese Buddhist tradition distinguishes a place that houses sacred relics from one that houses images and other sacred objects. Inside the Japanese pagodas are images and scenes from Buddhist lore and mandalas. Japanese pagodas became elaborate when Mahayana Buddhism was at its peak. The number of storeys increased to two, then five, seven, eleven and finally to thirteen. Precious little is known about the earliest stages of the development of the Japanese pagoda. The railings and gateways have disappeared.

Five-element Stupa or *Gorinto*: In Japan, a *gorinto* is different from a stupa. It has five storeys representing the five elements. These five-element stupas are common all over Japan and are constructed on the remains of a body. They corelate to the five elements to which the body returns after death, the five colours, and the five Buddhas of the Matrix World. A square stone represents earth, a round one water, a triangular one *tejas*, a hemispherical one air, and a flame- or jewel-like stone represents ether. The five-seed syllables – *a, vi, ra, hum,* and *kham* in Sanskrit – are inscribed on the front, and there is an elongated *vam* on the back of each stone. *Vam* is the seed syllable of the sixth element – consciousness. Thus it represents the non-duality of physical phenomena and the mind.

Caves: Abodes of silence

Caves were mankind's earliest dwellings, where visual art was tried. Buddhists were the first to carve out temples and monasteries by enlarging and improving natural rock shelters. Indians began to cut rocks in the third century B.C. An outline was marked and the cutting began from the ceiling with sharp and heavy instruments. Solid blocks were left for pillars and other constituents till the floor was reached. The caves served as temporary retreats for the monks.

PRECEDING PAGES 24-25:

Bodhanath is the largest stupa in Nepal. It dwarfs the two- and three-storey houses built around it. The diametre of its ground plan exceeds three hundred feet and the stupa stands on a platform of twenty angles, *vinshati-kona*.

A five-storey stupa representing the five fundamental elements of the world. From the lowermost to the uppermost level they symbolise the EARTH, WATER, FIRE, AIR, and SPACE.

As it is said: *Dharmasya tattvam nihitam guhayam,* meaning the essence of dharma is housed in a cave. It is a place of silence, darkness, depth and solitude. The knower, knowable and the knowledge were hidden together in the lap of *shunyata*, void and the prayers vibrated in both the mind and heart. *Ahata nada* (sound produced by contact) became *anahata* (unbeaten sound) and created an atmosphere that suited the monks in meditation.

Inside the dim and dark caves, sculptors carved a divine world out of lithic masses, and painters touched the walls to create a refreshing atmosphere of heavenly bliss. Buddhas, Bodhisattvas, compassionate and awe-inspiring deities, *nagas, garudas,* hell, and heaven, flying goddesses and guardians were painted in full glory and dharma was bought to the caves by travelling monks.

Ashoka and his grandson Dasharatha ordered that hills be cut to carve out caves in Gaya, Bihar. In Eastern and Western Deccan, the rocks were soft; the desired shapes were easily given. Around 200 B.C., Buddhist art had made its presence in this region.

Stupas were luxuriantly carved with Buddha images; aniconism gave way to iconism. They served a dual purpose, being both a monastic dwelling and a sanctuary. Kanheri and Bhaja are outstanding examples. Their façades are remarkably carved, stupas are erected inside and in the front. Rows of round or octagonal columns stand inside the central halls, which were meant for congregations. A range of cells on three

TOURISTS THRONG THE CAVES AT AJANTA WHERE BUDDHIST MONKS MEDITATED TO GAIN ENLIGHTENMENT. THIS PLACE OF NATURAL GRANDEUR IS A GORGE CREATED BY THE WAGHORA RIVER IN MAHARASHTRA, INDIA.

28

sides was made for dwelling apartments. Monks drew inspiration from the Buddhas sitting in the deep cavities, as if emerging out of a void.

Bhaja, Bedsa, Karle, Junnar, Kanheri, Pitalkhora, and Ellora (all in Maharashtra) are a few examples of Buddhist cave art. The finished caves are a treasure for historians and art lovers; the unfinished ones too give an insight into the methods employed in the excavations. Excavations continued from the first to the eleventh century. The cave sculptures display perfect coordination between architectural planning and sculptural embellishment.

Ajanta caves: The Mahayana phase of rock-cut cave art is seen in Maharashtra at Ajanta. All-inclusive, there are thirty caves. Some are called *chaitya grihas* while others are *sangharamas* or places for the monks. They display two distinctive phases of Buddhist rock-cut architecture.

Ajanta was a centre of learning and meditation. It is the oldest rock-cut cave monastery and was filled with the spiritual resonance of prayers chanted by thousands of people through hundreds of years.

Cave no. 10 is believed to be the oldest. Most probably its decorations date from the first century B.C. to the first century A.D. Some of the originals are superimposed by later works. At times the paintings on the ceilings are quite different in design and style from the hall. Their arrangement consists of rectangular panels filled with decorative motifs.

The Bagh caves - Madhya Pradesh - were carved on a sandstone cliff. Their walls bear splendid paintings that have survived in a scrappy and scanty form. Cave no. 4 is the most ornamental. Twenty-seven cells are carved around the pillared hall, which with its doors and windows, looks lavish. The pillar brackets are partly carved and partly painted. Bands of scroll work and floral motifs are sculptured on the doorway. *Chaitya* windows are inset with heads. In one scene, musicians and dancers are followed by two grand processions. The figures are full of majestic grace. The modellings are soft and sensuous, the compositions are rhythmic, the overall impression is that of a highly developed artistic vision and great technical skill.

The style of Ajanta spread as 'Ajantaism' over the entire Asian Buddhist world. The famous paintings of Sigiriya in Sri Lanka are their contemporary. At Bamiyan in Afghanistan and Yun-kang in China the scale of cut rocks and dug caves was so grand unlike that of Ajanta.

Sigiriya caves: One of the most renowned rock-shelter monasteries, the caves are spread over a hundred hectares. King Kashyapa I converted them into a fortified palace in the fifth century. The murals in the caves portray female figures emerging out of clouds, as part of a procession including the queen of King Kashyapa's court and princesses. They are on their way to a Buddhist shrine and carry various objects and a variety of flowers. Court ladies wear short-sleeved jackets of a thin and fine material. Coronets, tiaras, and aigrettes crown their heads and flowers and ribbons adorn their hair and ears. Their necks, breasts, arms, and wrists are loaded with a plethora of heavy ornaments and bejewelled trinkets.

The physical beauty of the female figures at Sigiriya is like those painted in the Indian cave shrines, especially the maidens sculpted at Amaravati. The maidens have

Shakyamuni sitting crosslegged on Mount Meru, surrounded by four Bodhisattvas and two disciples. The depiction is from the Pinyang caves at Lung-men, China, carved during the rule of the Northern Wei dynasty in China.

heavy-lidded eyes, a sharp nose and full lips typical of Sri Lankan features. Usually a lady of high rank is attended by a lady-in-waiting who is dark skinned or of kindred blood. Each figure has been given a touch of individuality due to the different traits on their faces. Their postures bend forward, the half-closed eyes look downward and sideways, full of the graceful stance of servitude. Their greenish blue eyes are not Asian.

Different scholars interpret the murals differently. It may be that they depict ladies of the court going to a temple or *apsaras* emerging out of clouds. Possibly it is a procession of royal ladies or the women are engaged in water sports. It can even be a symbolic representation of clouds and lightening.

Bamiyan shelters: To the northwest of Kabul on the Silk Route, Bamiyan in Afghanistan was a great centre of Buddhist art and thought. The Silk Route was used by monks, philosophers, teachers, traders, wanderers, and even invaders. The caves at Bamiyan are carved out of a cliff known as Koh-i-baba, meaning Saint Hill.

Monks hailing from India, Iran, Gandhara, and Greece dwelt there as one community. They were the creators of the paintings on the walls of twenty thousand caves. The paintings, usually dated to the fifth-sixty century A.D., were done in the Asian fresco technique. Their decorations mark the fusion of Indian, Greco-Roman, and Persian styles and the emergence of the Central Asian style. Paintings decorating the niche of the 175-feet high Buddha at Bamiyan were close to the Ajanta style though they also corresponded to the Iranian style. The colossal Buddhas stood as wonders for the world.

Shakyamuni Buddha sitting in the posture of Turning the Wheel of Law with his disciples and Bodhisattvas in cave no. 4, niche 7 of the Maichishan complex (China) comprising 200 caves.

The style was modified by artists at various Buddhist centres in the oasis cities of the western desert and then it went to China. The philosophical undercurrent kept flowing. The Silk Route became the *sutra* and the art route.

As Buddhism spread into China in the first century, the Quici area soon became a Buddhist centre at the southern foot of the Tianshan mountains. Grottos were hewn out of a cliff on a stretch of 3.2 km and became known as the Kizil Thousand Buddha grottos. Their construction began in second-third century A.D. and took a thousand years to complete. Originally there were 236 caves. Those with a central pillar had front rooms, central rooms, and rooms at the back. Some caves with large statues had back rooms; some did not. Special caves with a square lecture hall were meant for discourses by holy monks. Caves built for monastic purposes had quarters for the monks and passageways.

Yun-kang caves: In the third century the Han dynasty disintegrated, civil war and distress prevailed. Power was captured by the Weis or the Toba Tartars by the end of the fourth century; they brought stability to the country. The Weis had ambitious plans to cut rocks, build Buddhist monasteries and house images as symbols of their power and glory. The site chosen by them was Yun-kang, 16 km north-west of Datong. Most of the grottos were completed between A.D. 460 and 494. More grottos were added later. They housed a treasure of 51,000 images.

The wisdom and artistic skill of the Chinese is displayed in an exhibition of beautiful modelling, colourful design and exquisite techniques. The sculptures at Yun-kang were brilliantly coloured with lapis lazuli, malachite green, orange, and red. The middle group of the grottos contained images of Buddhas. The walls, archways, and ceilings were filled with sculptured niches containing small images and flying figures all carved in accordance with Buddhist philosophy.

The Lung-men rock-cut caves have gained worldwide popularity. In 494, the Wei capital was shifted to Loyang from Ta-T'ung. It was the Valley of the Dragon Gate or Lung-men near the I river that became the hub of activities for 250 years. Hard and fine dark limestone and a variety of marbles were easily available; these suited the needs of the artists. The caves lie in both the eastern and the western faces of the valley. There are 1,352 grottos with 2,100 niches decked with around 97,000 images. Moreover, there were 3,680 inscribed tablets and 40 pagodas.

Two major periods of construction are traced: the period from A.D. 495 to 537 falls in the Northern Wei and from A.D. 638 to 705 in the early T'ang. There are some inscriptions and monuments from the Northern Ch'i and Sui dynasties, too. The style has influenced the grottos at Dun-huang.

Dun-huang caves: In the western-most part of China, a shadow of the classic Indian tradition persists in the sixth- and seventh-century caves at Dun-huang. Dun-huang, an oasis in the Gobi desert, is known to the world for the treasure preserved in its 492 caves built over a period of thousand years. Chinese techniques are tried on Indian types and iconography. The construction of the caves began in A.D. 366 in the city that lies in the Kansu province on the borders of Chinese Turkistan. Its strategic location on the Silk Route made it a thriving centre of trade and Buddhist activities. The greatness of the legacy lies in thousands of painted statues, 45,000 square meters of murals, sutras, and scrolls. They are a rich source for the study of the history of art, customs, costumes, and political and military affairs. This is the best preserved and richest cave complex in China. The rock was not fit for carving as it was at Yun-kang and Lung-men. Images were made by moulding clay over a core of wood and straw, then paint was applied.

One of the scenes in the Dun-huang caves depict Shakyamuni's victory over the monster Papiyan standing in foreign clothes with his sons. Three beautiful women are trying to lure the Buddha. Flying goddesses carry trays of flowers and fruits to offer them to the Tathagata. They dwell in heaven and collect the sweet nectar of different flowers and scatter blossoms from the sky. They can be divided into three main categories: five goddesses of dance, five goddesses carrying musical instruments, and five goddesses carrying material for worship.

Vast paradise scenes with lofty architecture and divine figures of varied status were painted to visualise life after death. When devotion to Amitabha gained popularity, depiction of his paradise, Sukhavati, became the most popular theme for painting at Dun-huang. Cave no. 139 is a splendid example that was painted in the second half of the eighth century. Souls reborn in the western paradise sit on lotus flowers in the ponds. Dancers swing to the music played by musicians in the foreground. Avalokiteshvara and Mahasthama-prapta flank Amitabha, who is seated on a multi-coloured lotus seat.

Maichishan caves: Another world-renowned cave complex comprising 194 grottos on the Silk Route in Kansu province is Maichishan. Its construction began after Dun-huang. The cave complex preserved 7,200 clay statues and over a thousand square metres of murals. It followed Chinese standards of architecture. The cave complex is divided into east and west due to the middle cones that had collapsed. The cave called 'Seven Buddha Hall' is the largest. The clay of these statues is surprisingly hard. The large statues are up to 10 metres in height while the smallest is 10 cm. Different stylistic characteristics can be observed in images from different periods. Some Buddhist figures look as dignified as emperors.

Indian temples: Devastated and deserted

Buddhist monuments from Kashmir to Tamil Nadu, from the eastern region to Afghanistan to Gujrat are witness to the fact that there was a vast empire of Buddhist centres of devotion and art. The earliest monuments gave shelter to the Buddha's followers in the present states of Uttar Pradesh and Bihar. Monasteries were built in Rajgriha, Shravasti, Kaushambi, and so forth. Monastic dwellings began as simple thatched bamboo huts.

Once a merchant in Rajgriha offered sixty dwelling places to the Buddha for the use of the *Sangha*. A monastic abode was built at Gandhakuti, and monasteries were often built on the outskirts of cities. Rules were laid down for construction so that they did not become places of luxury. Later, they served as highly organised educational institutions and academic centres of Buddhist learning. Nalanda, Odantapuri, Vikramshila, Texila, and Ratnagiri were some of them. Normally a monastic complex had dwelling rooms, private chambers, porches, service halls, halls with fire places, store houses, wells, sheds, bathrooms, tanks, and halls.

Bodhgaya, on the banks of the Niranjana river, near the ancient village of Uruvela celebrates the Enlightenment of the Buddha. A polished sandstone throne under the peepal (Ficus religiosa) tree was a place of pilgrimage for Emperor Ashoka who erected a shrine over the *vajrasana*. The Bodhi Tree was re-grown several times and the Seat of Enlightenment was reconstructed. The Mahabodhi temple erected at the foot of the Bodhi Tree housed an image of the Buddha on the throne that was kept vacant earlier. Sri Lankan King Meghavarma gifted a monastery at this place in the fourth century. In the twelfth century, Udayashri from Sri Lanka installed a Buddha image. A large number of pilgrims offered votive stupas or erected memorials while taking a pilgrimage to the sacred spot. The centre was deserted under the pressure of Muslim invasions. Monks had blocked the front gate with bricks and it was plastered for protection from vandals. The door was reopened later. The Burmese took a special interest in the preservation and glorification of the temple in the thirteenth century. The temple was in use till the fourteenth century and then fell into decay. Finally, repairs were undertaken in the nineteenth century.

Sarnath, the sacred place of the first sermon, was also selected by Emperor Ashoka for erecting a pillar and a stupa. A colossal image of the Buddha was installed during the Kushana period. The place became popular as an important centre of art during the Gupta period. Buddha images from Sarnath are honoured as works of religious art. Spiritual luminosity is combined with grace and beauty. An approximately 60 square feet main shrine, a massive brick structure, is surrounded by votive stupas and faces

east. Chapels on the three sides of the outer walls are designed to contain images. Hiuen-tsang mentioned the existence of a 200-feet temple and a life-size bronze image of the Buddha in the *dharma-chakra-pravartana-mudra*. Many images of the Mahayana pantheon were discovered from there.

Nalanda, in Bihar, was visited by the Buddha several times as the mango tree grove, Pavarika, was his favourite halting place. The Gupta kings also built a number of monasteries and temples there. An 80-feet copper image of the Buddha, six-story temple buildings, an educational institute of world fame, its rich library and hostel that could accommodate ten thousand students, world-renowned teachers and philosophers gave it an honourable position in the history of education. Royal patronage given by the Pala kings raised it to greater prosperity. Teachers from the Nalanda University went to various Asian countries. Extensive excavations tell of the glory that lasted till the twelfth century.

Indonesian temples

Central Java was the cradle of cultural activities. Hillside sanctuaries were built in high remote areas. The stepped pyramid is one of the features of temples called *chandis*. A *chandi* was not able to accommodate large gatherings. There were many structural differences; some courtyards of *chandis* housed mortal remains.

A gray dark hard volcanic rock was used for their construction and the walls were covered with a 'diamond plaster' that was coloured and adorned. Existing *chandis* are reconstructions.

Indonesian art during the Hindu-Buddhist period took a sudden leap in technical and aesthetic achievement, and was remarkably accomplished in sculpture, architecture, poetry, and literature. Indian cultural elements were never adopted at face value. They underwent a certain varied degree of selection, modification, and remoulding. The oldest standing structures are all religious. They are places to pay homage to ancestors and to royalty in divine forms. Feverish building activity resulted in a large number of *chandis* in Java.

Chandi Kalasan, built to the east of Jogyakarta, stands on a flat undecorated foundation in an eighth-century style. According to the inscription it is dated 778,

Mahabodhi temple at Bodhgaya is a prototypic tower stupa with ancillary towers in the four directions that form a mandala. The formula is repeated at the summit of the tower. The original construction goes back to the sixth century. The present structure was, however, built in the thirteenth century and restored by the Burmese in the nineteenth century.

Chandi Plaosan in Central Java, Indonesia. A Shailendra princess and her husband Rakai Pikatan built the temple in the ninth century. The two storeys have an imitation third storey; each level has three rooms as in Chandi Sari.

~

dedicated to Goddess Tara and was commissioned by a Shailendra king. The wide terrace around the base of the temple enhances its vertical quality. An entrance porch leading into the cella projects from the central part of the façade. The central cell is surrounded by four subsidiary cells in projections, they have their own entrances. The inside chapel in the façade acts as an antechamber of the central cella. The *Kala*-head, often filling the space above the doors to protect the sacred building from the evil eye, is topped by a relief depicting the pointed temple roof.

Chandi Mendut, another monument of the eighth-ninth century, is situated three km east of Borobudur. It was built around an earlier monument. Re-embellishment and re-enlargement of existing monuments is a known feature of Indian and ancient Indonesian architecture. The original height of the temple should have been 26.5 metres

with a 12-feet tall foundation. It consists of a large *dagob* on the top surrounded by 8, 16, and 24 smaller ones on the lower levels. The walls are decorated with Bodhisattvas and gods. The suppleness of figure is admirable in high relief and sensitive carving. The decoration of the flight of steps is very different from others; a number of small panels are arranged like pictures in a gallery that illustrate the *Jataka* stories.

Borobudur has enriched the cultural heritage of Asia. Standing on nearly 403 square feet, it is the most prominent structure from the reign of the Shailendras. Borobudur, a gray silence of endless stone relief, enshrines the vision of a king in an ecstasy of form. Situated near Gunung Wukir, in the heart of mountains surrounded by volcanoes, it goes twelve centuries back. In A.D. 800, a king of the Shailendra dynasty immortalised his faith by building the structure that was conceived and concretised by a poet, thinker, and architect named Gunadharma. He meditated, went through great Buddhist classics representing the triple time of past, present, and future and conceived of Borobudur as known today.

Boro means *vihara, budur* means a hill, the word thus means a monastery on a hill. However, no inscription has been found there. The monastery is a fabulous summary of art and science visualised in a stepped pyramid crowned by a stupa. The first five galleries are richly decorated, niches house Buddhas; *dagobs* and minor ornamentation

Shakyamuni is sitting in the *Dharma-chakra-pravartana-mudra,* the posture of Turning the Wheel of Law at Chandi Mendut in Central Java. He is flanked by two Bodhisattvas - Padmapani and Vajrapani.

fills the rest of the space. A processional path formed by a heavy wall of stones surrounds them. Five galleries support three circular terraces adorned with seventy-two small *dagobs* arranged in three concentric circles. These circles surround a large *dagob* on a circular base devoid of any other decoration. There are no clearly marked entrances. Steps on four sides lead to the top.

The final stupa is bigger than all others, and is the crowning of the Vajradhatu Mandala. The crown of the monument is placed on a double lotus. It is closed firmly, the inside is an open space; this emptiness or *shunyata* is the absolute, the moment of silence, the highest expression of truth in the pilgrim's quest. A devotee ascends to Borobudur; on the higher terraces, he proceeds to the higher domains of spiritual life. The Tathagata manifests himself downwards in order to be approachable to beings. It is the descent of the divine to earth.

During the past centuries, Borobudur has been a victim of neglect, volcanic eruptions, and the ravages of climate. It collapsed and was remembered no more. From 1814, efforts were made to preserve Borobudur. Full-scale restoration was undertaken from 1907 to 1911 by Dr Van Erp. Since 1950s serious symptoms became evident: slanting of walls, rain water flowing through uncemented blocks of stones, eroding sculptures, stone relief being mercilessly split, and lichen infections inducing stone cancer. To avoid a total collapse, the Indonesian Government and UNESCO undertook restoration. Many countries pooled in with their resources.

One of the Buddhas sitting in the open at Borobudur, Central Java. Such images were placed inside the perforated stupas seen behind and built on the circular terraces that represent the world of form, *Rupadhatu*.

Borobudur is a replica of three large divisions of Buddhist cosmology. It demonstrates the ways in which the ultimate reality manifests itself in this three-fold world: *Kamadhatu, Rupadhatu,* and *Arupadhatu.* In the *Arupadhatu* sphere, no decorations or relief are needed. The highest is entirely abstract – formless, *arupadhatu.* The second is the sphere of forms, *rupadhatu;* and the third, *kamadhatu,* is the phenomenal world in which we live. Buddhas enclosed by the latticed *dagobs* of the circular terraces represent a transitional stage, partly visible and partly invisible in the *dharma-chakra-pravartana-mudra.*

Japanese monasteries

The noblest structures of Japan were constructed during a span of 700 years from the sixth to the thirteenth century. Many of them were built near Nara and Kyoto. The sculptures that are housed there are in perfect harmony with architectural surroundings and bathed in an atmosphere of sanctity and faith. These majestic buildings are reflections of the taste of their age and correspond to parallel developments in religion.

The Japanese imported the technique of building temples from Korea, which was based on the Chinese models of palaces. A Buddha hall was seen as a state throne, implying a similarity between the architecture of palaces and temples. The sixth century was a period of imitation and absorption. Gradually, the Japanese began to modify Chinese and Korean models into a uniquely Japanese style. The first and the supreme examples of temples based on Korean models are Asukadera and Shitenno-ji. The plans of Kawara-dera and Horyuji are inspired by the Chinese style of palace architecture. According to the Korean plan, a pagoda, a major hall of worship, the *kondo,* and a lecture hall were arranged on the same axis as the south and middle gates. But, according to the other plan used in Horyuji, a pagoda and a *kondo* are not arranged on the main axis.

By the year 624, during the regency of Prince Shotoku-taishi, 46 temples had been built. Some parts of the largest of these temples, Horyuji still stand intact – miraculously. The main building of the temple, the oldest example of a wooden structure worldwide, preserves the finest examples of early Buddhist art in Japan.

A pagoda and a major hall of worship are the focal points of Japanese temples. They are enclosed by a corridor, separating the world of the sacred from the profane. The words temple and monastery are used as synonyms. A pagoda might be a single-storey or multi-storey structure. The next in importance is a lecture hall built for the purpose of religious ceremonies, discourses, and meditation. Living quarters and refectories were essential for monks to live. Devotees and scholars used to gather at temples to expound Buddhist *sutras.*

Horyuji was built by Prince Shotoku-taishi together with his aunt, Empress Suiko, in pursuance of his father's will. The temple is one of the seven great temples of Nara and headquarters of the Sanron and Hosso sects, situated to the southwest of Nara. It is a treasure house of magnificent pieces produced during various periods. Two hundred artefacts are under state protection and the rest are Important Cultural Properties. The temple comprises of two sections, namely, the Sai-in or West Temple

A LAMA stands before the ornate door of a monastery. The stark landscape of high mountainous areas is often relieved by the rich colours of such Buddhist architecture.

and the To-in or East Temple. In 36 acres, there are 45 important structures (31 in the Sai-in and 14 in the To-in), of which 17 are registered as 'National Treasures' and 28 are Important Cultural Properties.

The front gate was rebuilt in 1439. Five pillars support the middle gate that divides the entrance into two parts. It is believed that the eastern entrance is meant for the living to visit the temple, while the western one takes the dead to paradise. Two fearful guardians stand in the niches on both sides of the gate. The right one is red and the other is black: they symbolise light and darkness respectively. The inner walls of the major hall bear murals depicting paradise scenes. Shakyamuni and Bhaishajayaguru are the main objects of worship made by a Korean sculptor. Four heavenly guardians stand on the four corners of the platform.

A five-story pagoda with its overhanging eaves draws graceful lines; the nine rings on the top are charms against thunderbolts. Inside the pagoda are four scenes: a discourse between Manjushri with Yuima, the division of Shakyamuni's relics, his entry into nirvana, and the paradise of Maitreya. The other important buildings in the temple complex are a lecture hall, a hall for cultural properties, a scripture house, and a belfry.

Ginkakuji or the temple of the Silver Pavillion in Kyoto, Japan, was formerly known as Jishoji. It was originally the palace of Ashikaga Yoshimasa (1436-90); after his death, it was converted into a Zen temple of the Rinzai sect.

All the buildings are National Treasures. Another attraction in the Horyuji complex is the Chuguji, which is situated to its east.

Todaiji in Nara is famous for the colossal image of Vairocana enshrined in its main hall of worship. The temple was founded in A.D. 728 for the repose of the spirit of Crown Prince Motoi, the son of Emperor Shomu. Rituals for national peace and prosperity were held there and monks were trained in its precincts. Many of its halls and gate structures were destroyed by quakes or burnt by fire, but were rebuilt. Today, the temple is a precious cultural treasure of paintings, sculptures, architecture, and Buddhist rituals.

The main hall at Todaiji is called Daibutsu-den. The oldest structure is the hall, Hokkedo. Hokke-e, or the ceremony of the Lotus Sutra, was held there. Splendid works of the eighth century are housed in this hall. The central figure is of Amoghapasha Avalokiteshvara flanked by two Bodhisattvas in the *anjali mudra*. There is a pair of goddesses, Sarasvati and Shri-Mahadevi; another pair of Sun and Moon gods; four Divine Guardian Kings and Vajradharas. All the images display great beauty and the artistic skills of the Japanese. Several other halls are important parts of the monastic complex. A repository is also attached. Chambers in the north and the centre

Kinkakauji or the Golden Pavillion in Kyoto, Japan, stands in a pond. Its original name was Rokuon-in-den, meaning a place where the Buddha preached for the first time. Today, it is a Zen temple.

hold the prized possessions of Emperor Shomu. The south chamber keeps ritual implements used in the annual ceremonies at Todaiji.

Daianji, Yakushiji, Gangoji, and Kofukuji are the other great temples of the Nara period, built in approximately thirty years between 710-740. Yakushiji is dedicated to the Buddha of healing and stands southwest of Nara. Built in the eighth century Shin-yakushiji is also situated southwest of Nara. Muroji is in the southeast of Nara and was established at the end of the eighth century as a mountain temple. It represents a harmonious simplicity in plan. Many wooden statues displaying austere expressions are from the early Heian period (A.D. 794-894). Toshodaiji is next door to Yakushiji. It displays grandeur of expression and its sculptural skill is best revealed in its excellent lacquer statues.

The Heian period saw further Japanese influence on architectural forms and led to fresh creativity. With the introduction of Shingon and Tendai sects, the entire arrangement of the various temple halls became irregular because the monk-scholars, Kobodaishi and Dengyodaishi, preferred to locate their temples in isolated grounds, on mountain tops or deep forests.

Kyoto, the capital of Japan from the late eighth to the twelfth century, is a city of temples. One of the most beautiful temples among them is Sanju-san-gen-do, a temple that enshrines one thousand life-size standing images with a seated image of the Thousand Armed Avalokiteshvara at the centre.

When the Japanese capital was shifted from Nara to Kyoto in the eighth century, two huge temples were built to protect the city. One was named Toji and the other Saiji. Toji houses a large number of Buddhist statues, carvings, paintings, and artistic handicrafts that were brought from China. The pagoda at Toji is the largest in Japan measuring 187 feet. Bhaishajyaguru in the main hall of worship looks full of mercy. He is attended to by the Sun and the Moon, and his twelve generals stand under his seat. There are twenty-one images in the lecture hall. The monasteries were meant for secret rituals, their construction was a reaction against the colossal and overpowering halls of Nara as they assumed an unadorned simplicity.

Enryakuji near Kyoto was established by Saicho (A.D. 767-622). Its central sector was a monastic complex with roofs covered with shingles made of cypress bark. Kongobuji established by Kobodaishi at Koyasan has lost many sacred images, but a considerable number have been preserved. Jingoji, on the northwestern corner of Kyoto, was built in A.D. 824. It is a Mikkyo centre of learning, also known as Takaosanji. Lacquer and wooden images of Bhaishajyaguru and five images of Akashagarbha Bodhisattva housed there are remarkable.

Hoo-do and Konjiko-do are the centres of the Pure Land devotional sect in the southeast of Kyoto. Their main object of worship is Amitabha. The workmanship is exquisitely Japanese. By the end of the Heian period, brilliant colours re-emerged in temple architecture. The style became decorative, endowed with subtleties, creating a unique beauty. This was the architecture of Pure Land Buddhism in which the Amida Hall was of central importance and catered to the need of esoteric performances.

The Burmese legacy

A hundred years after the Buddha's passing away in 444 B.C., Buddhism was established in the kingdom of Shrikshetra in Burma for 600 years. The kingdom of Pagan came into existence in A.D. 156 when 700 years after the Buddha's *parinirvana*. A city wall and a moat were built in about A.D. 850. Tripitaka, the Buddhist treasure of knowledge, was obtained from Sri Lanka in A.D. 1070 by King Aniruddha. One of the early temples built inside the walls was Pahto-thamya. Aniruddha was the Champion of Buddhism. The encryptions of Aniruddha are Buddhist prayers he signed on terracotta votive tablets with engravings of Buddhas and Bodhisattvas in the *Bhumisparsha Mudra* sitting on lotus seats which were used for stamping. Dozen of such seals have been recovered from various parts of Burma.

Aniruddha tried for overland contacts with East Bengal and Arakan to obtain Buddhist texts. Failing, he turned to the south and marched to Shrikshetra. Aniruddha laid the foundation of a number of stupas. His reign was of prime importance in the evolution of Pagan temples. He had brought architects, artists, masons, moulders, blacksmiths, silversmiths, filigree-flower workers, doctors, trainers of elephants and horses, makers of shields and other men skilled in various activities. The Tripitaka and the sacred relics were brought from there and the relics were kept in a bejewelled casket.

A glorious period of Buddhist architecture begins with the accession of the King Aniruddha to the throne in A.D. 1044 and his conquest of Lower Burma. At least 40 square miles of Pagan city formed the centre of the embellishments. Architects from Pegu, Prome, Thaton, and Arakan worked for the projects. Over the centuries a large number of monuments were destroyed. The monuments that survive are excellent examples of Burmese Buddhist art. There are stupas, sanctuaries with internal rooms and corridors, monasteries, and caves.

Massive temples were built on high pyramidal platforms while small temples consist of a simple sanctuary with a vestibule in the front and the main entrance at the far end. Their heights range from 10 to 200 feet. The main materials used were wood, brick, and stone. Little woodwork survives today. Good quality stone was rarely used for a whole construction. Normally it was used to strengthen brick work. The most brilliant and costly part was a metal fhinial usually made of a mixture of gold, mercury, and copper. The spire in the Burmese stupa was mostly a lotus. In a stupa, relics were placed in a sandalwood casket. Outside it was a casket of crystal, then one of sandalwood, another of gold and, finally, a casket of silver embossed with gems.

Old-style temples at Pagan are often single storied and asymmetrically planned. The block is square with a recess for the image. It is always dark and windows are made up of perforated stones or bricks. The corridors are dim and the inner shrine that

The Burmese pagoda in Pegu, east of Rangoon, is an example of a terraced stupa. Burma is the land of golden pagodas, hollow as well as solid. In terraced stupas, the dome is raised upon a podium.

contains the main image is pitch dark, based on the concept of a cave, a *guha*, and a *garbhagriha,* the central room.

The chief distinction between a Pagan temple and stupa is that the temples have an accessible interior space housing one or more images of the Buddha while the stupas are solid structures around which people can walk without any access to the interior. Small cavities sheltering relics are concealed in the core. The *shikhara* (temples with huge tapering summits) temple of Pagan consists of a cube topped by tiered terraces, crowned by a square tower with a curved profile, an analogue with the towers of Orissan temples. Some temples culminate in the dome and the spire of a stupa rather than a *shikhara*. Access to the inner space is indicated from the outside by a porch.

43

Among the temples and monasteries, well-known designs display a central shrine under a cloistered vault. There may be a corridor around a shrine. Temples are built on circular plans around a square solid core.

The Abeyadana temple, is in Pagan and was built by the wife of King Kyanzittha. Three entrances lead to the sanctuary that has a central pillar supporting the sloping roof and an enclosed corridor. Perforated stone screens let the light in. A niche carved in the north of the central pillar contains a Buddha image made of brick and stucco, seated in the *dharma-chakra-pravartana mudra*. Alongside the temple is a pagoda of the same period, which was a part of the shrine.

The lovely Abeyadana bears the finest paintings of the period in its hall. It combines simplicity with grandeur. It has a hall and a main block with corridors and a dark sanctum sanctorium, the image is place in darkness to represent the concept of *garbhagriha* as in cave and temple architecture. The hall is mutilated, the entrance porches have lost their pediments. Life-size paintings of standing *yaksas* on the side archways of the entrance porch come close to the concept of fertility emblems at Bharhut and Sanchi. There were two guardian Bodhisattvas to the left and right of the archway, but now only their pedestals remain. No niches exist in the hall for images. Complete sets of *Jataka* stories are painted in eight tiers. The outer wall of the corridor has plain niches between the windows. Stone statues that were mostly lost were originally placed in them.

Pahtothamya, an example of a stupa temple, was built during the reign of King Kyanzittha in the late eleventh century, though traditionally the date attributed to it is the tenth century. It is the most beautiful of all the Mon temples in Pagan. The temple faces east. Three doorways of the large hall have prominent arch-pediments. The position, size, and content of the temple and its artistic eminence indicate that it is a royal monument. Its plinth mouldings are the noblest in Pagan and are derived from the profile of a simple pot. Each of the three sides of the main block project a medial bay with perforated windows. Two more windows are there on each side of the bay. The apertures in the windows are round or square. All surface beauty is lost, windows are not ornamented, there are no pediments, friezes, or *dados*. The temple's *shikhara* is simple but unique. The *chhatravali* has twelve sides like the plinth descending into a square. The main dome has twelve foliated ribs rising up. The roof of the hall is broad and flat. The two upper roofs are sloping. Scenes from the life of the Buddha fill the main panels on the outer walls of the corridor: the nativity, the prophecy of Kaladenila, eight *brahmanas* examining the auspicious signs of baby Siddhartha, Gautama seated with attendants, his renunciation, Sujata offering him milk, Buddha drinking the milk, and so forth.

The Nanda temple, a masterpiece, depicts the climax of old Mon architecture and was the last monument King Kyanzittha built. It is spread, in full view of the city wall, from the end of the roof of the new palace built in A.D. 1102. Its reflection falls on a moat around the wall. A colossal image of the Buddha stands in full glory. The side niches have an image of a kneeling monk on the left and the king on the right. It is a perfectly symmetrical building and enshrines four Buddhas of the present *kalpa* (age). The scale of the temple is grand. A cube rises 160 feet in the centre to reach the spire. It has 52-feet high recesses in which stand four stately Buddhas made in wood, 32 feet in height on their eight-feet thrones. Two corridors, an outer and an inner, surround the central cube. Wooden doors on the four fronts divide the main temple from the four halls on the sides. All its terraces from top to bottom were once brilliantly inlaid with green glazed plaques. Those of the parapets above the corridors and halls present a bulk of *Jatakas*. It is the most complete series of *Jataka* plaques, numbering 1,464, at Pagan. Plaques on the ground plinth on the east depict gods celebrating the Buddha's triumph – a procession of *devas* and other mighty beings holding auspicious emblems. They include Suparnas, Nagas, Kumbhandas, Devas, and Devis, Yama, the king of death, the Regents of the Four Quarters, and Kubera, the Yaksa general with his retinue. Eighty scenes are carved on the walls of the outer corridor. Kneeling monks and King Kyanzittha attend to the Buddhas in the four shrines.

Thai temples

Thai temples are peaceful resorts of divine grandeur. The construction and donation of religious buildings was an act of merit for the Thais. Monumental temples and great monasteries of both the Mahayana and Theravada sects were the works of devotees and not professionals, so their art remains anonymous. A temple is a tangible link between the world of men and the world of gods. Every component of a temple complex has a symbolic meaning. Elements are not employed for decorative effect but to convey symbolic intent. The Thai architects modified them to fit them into their requirements in the most beautiful way. A *Bot, Ho Trai, Vihara, Phra Chedi, Phra Prang, Mondop, Prasat, Sala, Sala Kan Parien, Kuti* and so forth are the major buildings in a temple complex.

A group of various buildings enclosed by a wall with gates and meant for religious purposes is often called a *Wat*. Almost every *Wat* has a differently designed gateway. Elements in the Thai superstructure can be traced back to Indian Buddhist architecture. There can be one or three openings with triangular arches with the Naga motif harmonising with the main structure that has triangular gables. The superstructure of the gate of Wat Po in Bangkok is shaped like a royal Thai crown.

A *Bot* in a Thai temple corresponds to the Indian *Chaitya* Hall. Generally, a large *Bot* is built on a platform. Its plan is rectangular and enshrines a gilded image of the Buddha placed on a pedestal. Its interiors often receive limited light and the walls bear paintings. The size differs in accordance with functional necessities. Graceful finials of the *makara* (mouth of the crocodile) motif ornament the ridges of roofs. A *Bot* can have up to three doors. Its windows used to be narrow vertical openings during the Ayutthiya period (A.D. 1350-1767), but later a series of windows were opened with wooden panels. The exterior and interior pillars of *Bots* in old Thai architecture were octagonal. Their capitals have lotus forms; the wooden ceilings were painted.

A *Vihara* keeps the Buddha's images; it is not a monastery, its size is lesser than a *Bot* in Central Thailand, but in the north this is reversed. It can be the main building in a complex standing in the centre of the courtyard, enclosed by a gallery that opens inside and is closed on the outside. The Buddha's images in stucco or bronze are placed along the gallery. Its walls can be decorated with paintings.

The buildings are principally made of laterite and brick covered with stucco. Wood was rarely used as the only material for the building. It was used for roofing brick buildings and for decorative and ornamental purposes when it was generally gilded and enriched with glass mosaic. Pillars and all other wooden and stucco ornaments were decorated with gilt, dark red, green, blue, and violet colours. Gilded ornaments in wood or stucco, architectural mouldings and stucco designs added to the glittering effect of the buildings. More decorative elements were added by the use of ceramic tiles. Glazed terracotta ornaments were used to decorate old temples. In the later periods, small pieces of porcelain from broken vessels were used to form ornamental patterns. Sometimes sandstone was used in lintels; slate was occasionally employed. Stone surfaces were finished and then painted or gilded. Stucco was extensively used to enrich architectural mouldings to model ornaments of window and door frames. Designs on doors and windows were done in gold while the surface was covered with black lacquer.

Art and architecture saw various phases of stylistic changes during the thirteenth-eighteenth century A.D. But the norms that governed them conformed more to tradition and saw less creativity. Each form was governed by textual sources or ritual needs. Learned monks who were ordained in Burma, brought different styles to Thailand. They visited Sri Lanka in search of religion, philosophy, sacred texts, and observe methods of creating magnificent centres of learning. When the Thai monk Sisatta returned from Sri Lanka he was accompanied by artists who introduced new methods and construction designs. The influence of Sri Lanka was the most profound. The Pala School of Indian art and the Pagan of Burma were also rich sources of inspiration for the Sukhothai artists. They adopted Burmese and Cambodian techniques for stucco works.

Wat Po or the Temple of the Reclining Buddha is one of the major attractions in Bangkok. It is the oldest and the largest of all the *Wats*. The compound is packed with chapels, pavilions, and *Chedis*. There are rows upon rows of gilded Buddhas. Episodes from the *Ramayana* are depicted on marble bas relief on the walls of the *bot*. Four large *Chedis* commemorate the first four kings of the Chakri dynasty. A 150-feet statue of the reclining Buddha is the focal point.

The temple of the Emerald Buddha in Bangkok was built by King Rama I when he established his capital and named it Ratnakaushin in 1782. He built the Royal Temple within the palace. It is popularly known as Wat Phra Kaeo meaning the residence of the Gem Buddha. Its enclosure galleries bear mural paintings depicting the story of Rama. The convocation hall for the Buddhist clergy is meant for the monks' recitation of disciplinary regulations and confessions. It is also the place where new monks are ordained. The image of the Emerald Buddha is enshrined in the wooden hall with a multi-story roof. The boundary is marked by sacred stones called the *Bai Sema*. There are several open pillared halls meant for the laity and for the recitation of tales. *Phra Chedi* or the *Chaitya* is an object of veneration. Two more golden *Chedis* have been built there by King Rama I in memory of his parents. Another hall meant for the assembly houses a beautiful image of Lord Buddha. The laity can come and perform ceremonies there. Two repositories are built for keeping the *Pali Tripitaka*. Building a library was considered a meritorious act; the younger brother of the king built one to keep Buddhist texts.

Ayutthiya, a sacred city located fifty miles from Bangkok, is known as Phra Nakhon Sri Ayutthiya. It was established as a capital city in the fourteenth century by Ramadhipati and was ruled by thirty-three kings of five dynasties. It was one of the most illustrious cities with three glorious palaces and 400 glittering temples. The Ayutthiyan period was the apex of art in Thai history. Sukhodaya was the rival kingdom of Ayutthiya. The grand temples of Ayutthiya faced large-scale destruction by the Burmese who sacked Ayutthiya in 1767. Today, the ruins of the monumental achievements lie scattered. Huge parts of sculptures that once adorned their interiors can be seen lying in the open.

Wat Phra Sri Sanphet was the royal temple that once stood within the compound of the King's palace. It was built in 1448 and was restored twice. Some of its *Chedis* are restored to reflect Ayutthiyan-style architecture. Quite close to this is Vihar Phra Monkon Bopit which houses a gigantic Buddha image. The building is newly built to match its earlier glory. To its southeast is Wat Phra Ram. Another astonishing construction was identified by its large central *Prang*; this was built by the second king of Ayutthiya at the site of his father's cremation. Wat Mahathat, Wat Rachaburana, Wat Wat Na Phra Mane and a large number of other temple complexes are still centres of devotion for the Thais. They wrap the stupas in Ayutthiya in monk's garments as a sign of their dedication.

The rulers of Ayutthiya were exceptional builders. The great monuments at Ayutthiya display certain characteristic features of temple architecture. They follow different types of plans and use imperishable materials in temple construction. Extraordinary examples of artistic beauty and symbolism, the influence of Burmese and Sinhalese architecture can be easily traced in them. Resemblance to the Khmer style is evident in central *Prangs* and open courtyards.

PRECEDING PAGES 46-47:
THE DALAI LAMA'S ROOM IN THE POTALA PALACE built by THE SECOND DALAI LAMA IN 1645 AT LHASA, THE CAPITAL OF TIBET. LHASA literally MEANS 'DIVINE LAND'. THE word POTALA IS derived from *POTALAKA*, SOUTHERN PURE LAND, THE EARTHLY abode of AVALOKITESHVARA.

A ceremonial dance being performed in front of a Buddhist temple.

Following pages 50-51:
Tashi Lhumpo monastery in Tibet was a monastic university in Shigatse, Tsang, founded by the first Dalai Lama in 1445. The monastery was divided into forty wards placed under the jurisdiction of three collegiate schools. Currently, it is the seat of the Panchen Lamas.

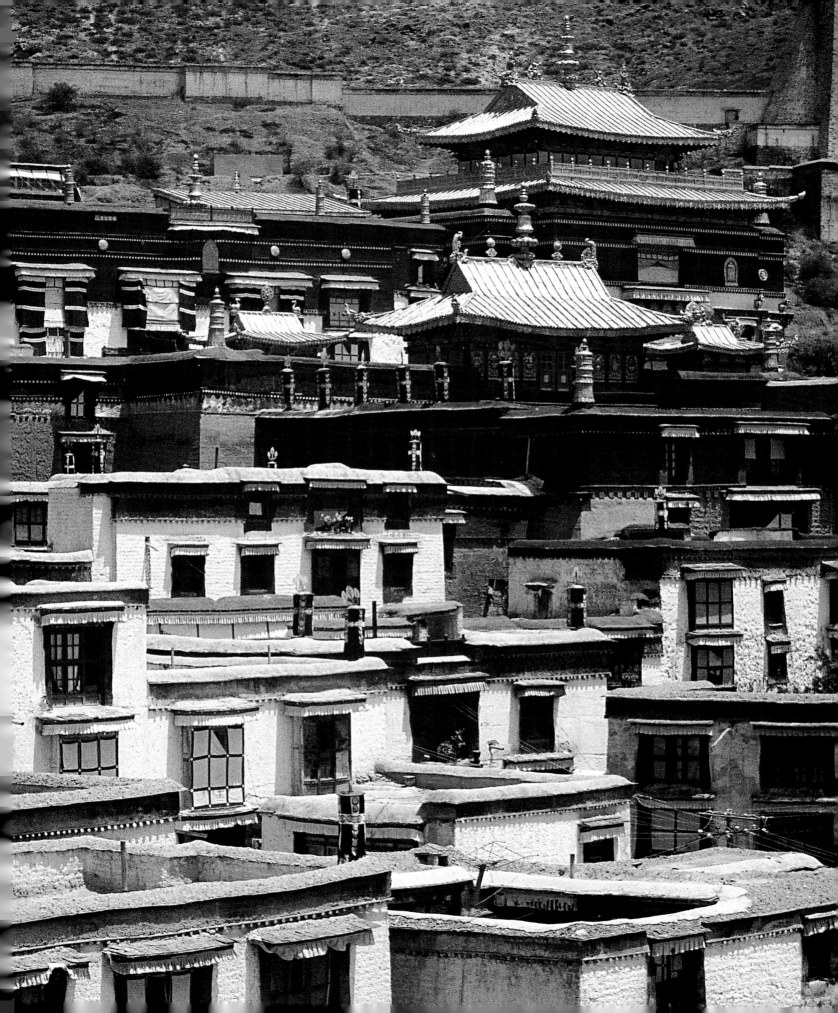

Maitreya Bodhisattva from Gandhara in grey schist from the the Kushana period (second-third century A.D.). Maitreya is sitting crosslegged on a cane seat, *betrasana*, holding a vase in his hand. The broken hand should have been in the posture of fearlessness, the *Abhaya Mudra*.

Sculpture: Iconic representation

Different forms of the Buddha

Followers and devotees, kings and laymen glorified and worshipped the Buddha as a divine teacher. They sought inspiration from the events of his life. However, he was venerated in an aniconic form. Carvings in *stupas* at Bharhut and Sanchi made in the second and third century are the earliest examples of aniconic symbolism. The stupas are surrounded by a vertically and horizontally divided railing decorated with the lotus wheel or a medallion in relief that represents donors or aniconic scenes from Buddha's life. The *torana* at Sanchi is crowned by a wheel. Male and female fertility deities, tree and woman motifs are incorporated. Groups of worshippers are visualised as adoring the symbols of the Buddha.

A wheel was carved to represent the first sermon and a *stupa* to worship the relics of the Buddha. The articles used by him and his footprints were also objects of adoration. Aniconism was transformed into anthropomorphism by the reliefs at Bharhut, Sanchi, Bodhgaya, and Amaravati. The Buddha's mother and attendants, disciples and adorers, Chandaka and others were represented in iconic forms. This paved the way for the Mathura and Gandhara schools of art. Moreover, the Greeks had made images in northwestern India. A little later, sculptors began to carve the images of the Buddha. Within a few generations, all the Buddhist sects took to worshipping images. The Buddha was worshipped as a Lord even in Theravada monasteries. He was offered flowers, fruits, incense, and other things.

The earliest known representations of the Buddha are found on the coins of the time of King Kanishka. On them, the Buddha stands, preaches, or meditates. Sanskrit inscriptions from the first to the third century A.D. record that images of Buddhas and Bodhisattvas were given as gifts. *Sutras* speak of making images in the Buddha's absence after his departure to the Trayastrinsha heaven, the second of the six heavens atop Mount Meru in Buddhist cosmology. The *Ashta-sahasrika-prajna-paramita*, a Buddhist text, reveals that a Buddha image was made shortly after his death.

A free-standing image of Shakyamuni from Gandhara in the collection of the National Museum, New Delhi. Models for the Gandhara school images were provided by Greek divinities, and Hellenistic technical details are obvious in their execution.

His statues began to appear in Gandhara and Mathura. He was presented as the Enlightened One and the Perfect One. There are two precedents at Mathura for these images: the first has a figure sitting contemplatively as a *yogi*, an ascetic; the other stands with his right arm raised and the left bent at the waist. In Gandhara, Western art influenced Buddhist art. The architectural decorations reveal a direct Hellenic influence. The Buddha is present there figuratively as a teacher as at Mathura. By this time, the Bodhisattvas had begun to appear, too. The first among them is Maitreya, who waits in Tushita heaven (the paradise of Maitreya) to descend on Earth, to redeem the world from suffering.

Birth of the Buddha: Queen Maya left for her parents' home when she was expecting. She had only reached the park of Lumbini, when she bore her child. Two maids were with her. She held on to a branch of a sala tree to bear the pain. Bodhisattvas, Indra, and Brahma came to escort the child. The new-born was given a bath and he walked seven paces towards the four directions of the compass, exclaiming: 'This is my last incarnation.' The momentous event provided sculptors, painters, and artistes with a theme.

Infant Shakyamuni: Bronzes of Shakyamuni at the time of his birth are placed in Buddhist monasteries in basins. His birthday is celebrated on the eighth day of the fourth month of each year. The Buddha is an infant but his image looks mature to denote his inner wisdom. He raises up his right hand and points down with the left to proclaim his domain. In Japan, sweet tea is poured over the image which is taken out of the basin by the devotees on the birthday. The earliest known such image is from Todaiji in Nara.

Buddhas in *bhumisparsha mudra*: Shakyamuni sits in the *bhumisparsha mudra* or the posture of Touching the Earth, calling her to give witness to his enlightenment. The gesture was occasioned when the Buddha was sitting under the Bo tree. Mara with his immeasurable demons was trying his best to tempt him to take nirvana or moksha and leave mankind behind with its suffering sores. The Buddha sat in a serene and motionless state, he was aware of the causes of sufferings and also of the way to attain liberation. Unaffected by Mara, he called on the Earth with his right hand and all the demons were destroyed.

According to another legend, since the Buddha got enlightenment in solitude, where he had no other witness to confirm the event, he called on the impartial mother of all, the goddess Earth. She emerged from the ground near the place where the then Bodhisattva was sitting and said: 'It is as you say, I am the witness.'

A large number of Buddhas sitting in the *bhumisparsha mudra* are found in Buddhist countries, especially in Theravada countries like Thailand, Cambodia, Sri Lanka, and Burma. Colossal statues in Thailand remained popular in the history of Thai Buddhist art. A marble image from Burma can be taken as an

The Buddha as an infant. The image is from the Todaiji monastery in Nara, Japan. He is raising up his right hand and pointing down with the left to proclaim that he is the ruler of heaven and earth. Such images are worshipped during the birthday celebrations of the Buddha in Japan.

Ushnisha-Vijaya, the Goddess of Supreme Victory, from Mongolia by the most famous sculptor Zanabazar.

example. In Burma, marble was brought from the hills in the north of Mandalay or south of it from the seventeenth to the nineteenth century to carve out religious sculptures. The images were partly painted or gilded, details were added in lacquer. The hair curls are cut into stone but there is a bejewelled fillet around the hairline and the robe decorations are done in lacquer. Pieces of coloured mirror glass are inset. In almost all the Cambodian and Ayutthiyan style images, a broad band joining the forehead to the hair is the characteristic feature.

Much of the Buddhist stone sculptures of Burma show the characteristics of the Late or Post-Gupta style with Buddha figures often sitting cross-legged and wearing robes that cling tightly to the body. Bodhisattvas sitting in *rajalilasana*, wearing the sacred thread or *yajnopavita*, sporting an elaborate hairdo, and wearing coronets and jewellery can be stylistically compared to the early Pala period.

The art of Burma was mainly devoted to Theravada Buddhism. Seated Buddhas are often in meditation. Tight-fitting robes with flaps over the shoulders indicate a relationship with northeast India.

Buddha's descent from the Trayastrinsha heaven: Trayastrinsha represented the second of the six Buddhist heavens on the top of Mount Meru. The Buddha went there to meet his mother and preached the philosophy found in the Abhidharma, a Buddhist text. There in the Sudhamma meeting hall he sat on Indra's throne under the *parijata* tree, a characteristic of this particular heaven. The tree bears flowers that shine like the morning Sun. Petals lie scattered on the divine seats. The Buddha is sitting inside a building. A tree is to its right. Behind is the Chulamani Chaitya, where lies the lock of Buddha's hair that he had cut off at the time of renunciation, and the tooth that was placed in the same stupa by Shakra or Indra. In front is a jewel ladder that was made to bring down the Buddha to Sankissa. A shrine was built at the point where his right foot first touched the earth.

Buddha turns the Wheel of Law: This is the eleventh episode among the twelve in the life of the Buddha. When he was enlightened he decided to impart his teachings to the five ascetics whom he found in a Sarnath park. This is known as the first sermon or Turning of the Wheel of Dharma. The Buddha sat on a pedestal flanked by Brahma and Indra and five disciples listened to him. Hence on, for forty-five years he was constantly on the move with his disciples and his worshippers increased. Richly coloured wall hangings were produced for the temples that enact such scenes. Shakyamuni sits on the sacred throne surrounded by Bodhisattvas and disciples. Heavenly angels fly on the clouds. Embroideries based on the theme were also produced.

Shakyamuni's sermon from the Gridhrakuta mountain is another important theme. The Buddha sits in the *dharma-chakra-pravartana-mudra* flanked by Bodhisattvas Samantabhadra and Manjushri and surrounded by disciples. He is paired with Prabhutaratna by the followers of *Saddharma pundarika*, the Lotus Sutra. Both are seated inside a *stupa* set in paradise. A bronze plaque at the Hase dera monastery in Japan depicting this is the main object of worship. A thousand Buddhas fill its upper part and the lower is filled by an inscription with two guardian figures on the sides.

Buddha reclines for the final rest: The *Parinirvana* of the Buddha, the most moving subject in Buddhist art, has inspired a large number of masterpieces throughout the Buddhist world. The Parinirvana is the final episode of his life, occurring when the Buddha reached Kushinagar accompanied with his disciple Ananda and others. Ill, he sat between two sala trees and directed Ananda to prepare his couch. Ananda wept but obeyed his orders. The Tathagata laid down with his head towards the north, put his right hand beneath his head, and crossed his feet like a monarch. His followers gathered around, the wind hushed, the forest streams were silent, no sound was heard, trees sweat out large flowing drops, flowers and leaves fell mournfully. And he passed away. The great Earth quaked, the Sun and the Moon forgot to shine.

The *Parinirvana* of the Buddha is famous all over the Hinayana as well as Mahayana countries. Colossal reclining images were carved out of rocks in Bamiyan and other parts of Asia. In Bangkok an image of the Reclining Buddhas is housed in

the temple of Wat Po. The brick image is 150 feet in length. It is covered with plaster and gold leaf. The soles of the Buddha's feet are intricately carved, depicting auspicious signs inlaid with mother of pearl.

Buddha walks: The Sukhothai walking Buddha is an extraordinary example of innovation in what is the most complete visualisation of the *mahapurusha lakshanas* or the signs of divinity that a *mahapurusha* (Great or Divine Man, ubermensch) possesses. Artists of the Sukhothai period in Thailand created masterpieces that move with grace. The Teacher is advancing forwards to announce the doctrine. The body has a graceful undulation, hanging arms rhythmically follow the curve of the body. The head is shaped like a lotus bud. The neck merges harmoniously into the shoulder. Each detail is delicately outlined to emphasise the harmony of the whole composition. Hands are modelled with grace and elegance. Some images are so delicate that they appear somewhat feminine.

The Thai people consider Buddha images as living beings. They are offered food during feasts, given a bath during the New Year festival and given a shawl to protect them during winter. The Emerald Buddha has three changes of clothing corresponding to three seasons.

The reclining Buddha from Wat Chetupon, Bangkok. The gilded brick and stucco image is highlighted by enormous feet on which 108 auspicious signs have been crafted in mother of pearl.

Crowned Buddhas: The Buddha in royal attire, dressed as *rajadhiraj*, king of the kings, is the *sambhogakaya* form of the divine personality. According to legend, Jambupati held himself in such high esteem that he could not listen to the master. So the Buddha manifested himself as *rajadhiraj* and summoned Jambupati. The king was awe-struck by the splendour of the scene and paid obeisance to the Buddha, especially when he saw the open chasm before him issuing fire. He became his disciple and accepted his philosophy.

Crowned Buddhas wearing jewellery from the Pagan period are associated with royalty. They wear bands crossing over the chest similar to the ones worn by Burmese kings. Such images were found in Shrikshetra, Pagan, and Pegu. According to Pali commentaries, the Buddha took on the form of a king to preach to the kings. The flame-shaped *ketumala* is a conspicuous hallmark of the Sukhothai Buddha images as well as those from south India and Sri Lanka.

Buddhist portrait sculptures: The grand temples of Indonesia and the images housed there represent the dual principal of religion and politics, the apotheosis of kings, a symbiosis of royalty and religion, humanity and divinity. At the time of political instability, ambitious dynasts sought transmission of divine grace unto them through the evocation of transcendental powers.

They resorted to religious activities to consolidate their political power, to glean the vitality of the spiritual forces. For a couple of centuries, the dedication of religious monuments was a testimony to the faith of the royal patrons in the transcendental source of power and legitimacy. Thus a large number of *chandis* in Indonesia served the purpose of ancestor worship.

Ancestor worship was a special task laid upon kings. They had to establish ritual contact with their ancestors to strengthen their position through magical powers received from them. Thus worship of posthumous images of kings in the form of Vishnu, Shiva, or Buddha became a fashion. Use of divine images for announcing political hegemony was another important step taken by Kritanagara in the thirteenth century. He sent an image of his father Vishnuvardhana to Chandi Jago to ensure contact between that kingdom, his vassal state, and his dynasty through the cult of ancestor worship. Moreover, the kings themselves claimed to rule as incarnations of various divinities.

Many conceptions of Buddha have given rise to a kaleidoscopic iconography. As a teacher he is either sitting or standing. The images of the Buddha are primarily composed by use of symbolic and spiritual elements. The artistic considerations enhance and sustain all the other values. The thirty-two signs of a Great Man *(mahapurusha)* are seen in early iconographic conventions. The Buddha, thus, has an *ushnisha*, a lock of hair curled up at the top of his cranium. The *urna* was a small round bump of flesh or a tuft of hair in the middle of his forehead that was to emanate light. Three rings of flesh encircle his neck, his earlobes are

Walking Buddha from Wat Benjima Bopit, Sukhothai, Thailand. The graceful movements of the teacher are an innovation of the Thai sculptors of Sukhothai (13th-15th century) that showcase their mastery in bronze casting.

Bottom:

Maitreya from Koryuji monastery, Kyoto, Japan. The Hakuho-style, seventh century image is made of wood. Bodhisattvas in the same meditative posture are found in Koguryo, Korea and Lung-men in China. According to the latest identification made by Prof Lokesh Chandra this image is of the monk Asanga.

The Bronze statue of Lord
Shakyamuni is from Ming China
(1368-1644). The Buddha is in
the Turning the Wheel of Law
posture and sitting in the
Vajrasana. The image is in the
National Museum, New Delhi.

exceptionally elongated, a thousand-spoked wheel is imprinted on his soles. His soft skin does not hint at roughness. His fingers are webbed. Following the *mahapurusha lakshanas*, his arms are exceptionally long and touch his knees. His body gleams, his halo emits light. In narrative scenes, he is often taller than others. Apart from the thirty-two auspicious signs, there are eighty subsidiary features of a superhuman that are added while painting or sculpting divine images.

Buddhas, as the manifestation of the Absolute, were depicted in regal vestments more often than in the monk's robes. The tendency increased with the passage of time because one of the attributes of kingship is victory and Buddha is a *Jina*, he who has won the great victory. So Buddha images were adorned with regal robes, crowns, necklaces, and other jewels. He is the Universal Monarch, the *chakravartin*.

Some statues have wings of flame at the shoulders. As the Buddha of Healing he is Bhaishajyaguru. There are Buddhas who sit and preach in full majesty. Amitabha is one of them; he has risen to the paradise of beatitude, Sukhavati. Another is Akshobhya, who is surrounded by the choirs of the blessed in Abhirati heaven and Maitreya, the Future Buddha in Tushita heaven.

Buddha images are identifiable through their attributes and characteristic features. Amitayus holds a vase containing the water of longevity. Shakyamuni often sits in *dharma-chakra-pravartana-*, *bhumisparsha-*, and *varada-mudra*. But nothing is fixed. Attributes and *mudras* differ in different traditions and texts. They symbolise various aspects. Preaching of the Law alludes to the revelation and availability of truth to man. Protection or assurance signifies that only Truth can free man from the cycle of rebirth. Touching the Earth refers to the certainty of possessing the Truth. Meditation recalls that without concentration Truth will not shine.

Each Buddha has his own throne or vehicle. Akshobhya rides an elephant, Vairocana a dragon, Amitabha a peacock, Ratnasambhava a horse and Amoghasiddhi a Garuda. They are distinguished through their colours also: Akshobhya and his family are blue, Vairocana is white, Amitabha is red, Ratnasambhava is yellow, and Amoghasiddhi green. Colour is an essential element in mystic symbolism. It replaces the splendour of gold. Buddha was of golden colour, and all the images were gilded because gold was the sign of resplendent spiritual luminosity.

In Japan, the Buddha is also worshipped as *Dainichi-nyorai*, as the polar star painted in white colour, wearing white garments seated on a lotus. He wears an ornate crown and sits in *dhyana mudra* with the tips of his thumbs joined.

Buddhas of three times

Dipankara, Buddha of the past: Dipankara is from *'deepa'* meaning lamp. He is the most celebrated and the first of the twenty-four Buddhas. Dipavati is the name of his capital city. In a past *kalpa*, King Arcishtra lived there. Dipankara was a Bodhisattva in Tushita heaven during the same *kalpa*. When the time came for him to descend he entered the womb of one of the spouses of the king as the king was thought most suitable to be his father. When the queen was in the throes of childbirth she asked the king to send her to a lotus pond. As soon as she reached the spot, an island sprung up in the midst of the pond for the Bodhisattva to take birth. A large number of bright lamps manifested miraculously.

FACING PAGE:

MAITREYA, THE FUTURE BUDDHA, FROM THE TASHI LHUMPO MONASTERY, THE LARGEST OF ITS KIND. COLOSSAL IMAGES OF JAM-PA OR THE LOVING ONE, MAITREYA, WERE OFTEN CARVED OUT OF ROCKS OR MADE OF CLAY AND THEN GILDED.

Dipankara Buddha is believed to have lived on this earth for 100,000 years. He kept on finding someone worthy of hearing the divine truth. Then he decided to convert the world and caused a miracle which appeared in the form of a great city that materialised from his lamp and became stationary in space. Fierce flames emitted from the four walls while the people of Jambudvipa gazed upon the miracle. Their hearts were filled with fear and they looked for Buddha to save them. Dipankara came forth from the burning city, descended, and seated himself on a lion to teach the law.

Like all other Buddhas, Dipankara has short curly hair, *ushnisha*, *urna*, and long earlobes. Sometimes his right hand is in *abhaya mudra*. When a triad is formed he is flanked by two Bodhisattvas. Dipankara has always been popular in China. Several examples can be seen in the cave temples of Yun-kang and of Lung-men.

Shakyamuni, Buddha of the present: Shakyamuni, the sage of the Shakyas, the historical Buddha known as Siddhartha was the founder of Buddhism. He was born in a Shakya clan family in the Nepalese Terai in Lumbini. He lived between 563-483 B.C. He is venerated as a Tathagata: one who has attained the essence of truth and as a *Jina*: one who has conquered. He became Buddha, one who has attained enlightenment, a heroic achievement. He got enlightenment at Bodhgaya, gave the first sermon at Sarnath, and attained nirvana at Kushinagar. He accepted rebirth and transmigration. According to him moral values are the result of deeds performed in previous years and *karma* makes one's life fundamentally painful and also conditions life.

Buddha is teacher in Hinayana Buddhism; his life is an example that everyone must follow. In the Mahayana path, he is a manifestation of the Truth and the Absolute. His word is the self-revelation of truth. He has an infinite number of colleagues; all reflections of the same truth. The concept underwent profound changes, and as a manifestation of self-revealing Supreme Existence, he became Shakyamuni. He was considered as the Buddha who is seen on celestial planes. Finally, he was seen as the Supreme Buddha.

Maitreya, Buddha of the future: Maitreya's association is with the Sun god Mitra. It is around him that the light cults came into being. They are represented by Amitabha, Vairocana, and Maitreya. He is also one of the Buddhas of the three times. Dipankara is the Buddha of the past, Shakyamuni of the present, and Maitreya of the future. Maitreya is said to be waiting for the time when he will

Amitabha Buddha, one of the colossal bronzes from the Kotokuin monastery, Kamakura, Japan. The monastery was burnt down and could never be reconstructed so the Buddha sits in the open.

descend to earth. He is the hope of civilisation expressing the invisible future by means of the visible. He confers happiness.

There are a variety of forms of Maitreya. The Maitreya may be portrayed sitting or standing, displaying various combinations of *mudras* and attributes. His cult was popular in the earliest centuries of the Christian era. Devotees hoped to be reborn in his paradise. The conception of him as the Future Buddha, endowed them with hope that if reborn they would be redeemed by his teachings.

Maitreya is generally golden in colour, peaceful and resplendent, sits in a *lalita* posture with both legs hanging, his matted locks are his crown, *jatamukuta*, he holds a twig of *nagakesara* flower in his right hand, and a miniature *chaitya* ornaments his hair. His heaven is called Tushita. In Tibet he is also represented as a Bodhisattva sitting in *bhadrasana,* wearing ornaments and a crown. Pendent legs indicate his readiness to descend on the earth, to establish the lost truth in all purity. Both his hands may be in the *mudra* of teaching or may hold a lotus, a *chakra* or a vase.

Two scholars flank Maitreya: Asanga and Vasubandhu. A Japanese philosopher of the Tendai school has said that the sunlight of Shakyamuni has been hidden in the distant clouds and we have not yet seen the glimpse of the moonlight of the merciful future Buddha, Maitreya. Maitreya descends from heaven and comes in a cloud featured like a rainbow. The ray of Maitreya that comes down from the top splits into five different colours, touches Asanga and ends its course in a white flame. So Asanga is white, an expression of his illumined consciousness. Asanga was a professor at Nalanda and spent much time in Ayodhya, a centre of learning. His younger brother was Vasubandhu. Vasubandhu was a scholar of philosophy. Their distinctive personalities are brought out in *thangka* paintings. Asanga is calm and serene while Vasubandhu is energised thought.

Shakyamuni Buddha sitting with his disciples and Bodhisattvas from the Lung-men caves in Hunan province, China. The depiction was carved in the seventh century A.D.

Buddhist colossi

Over the ages colossal images have been made by rulers all over the world to exhibit their power, their political or religious strength, and their will. The massive statue of Apollo Helios made from the melted down weapons of defeated enemies, one of the Seven Wonders of the World, symbolised victory. The Roman Empire erected colossal statues to impress the world with its might. In the Buddhist world, however, the statues were meant to inspire the devotee by the grand personality of Shakyamuni who was so majestic, overwhelming, strong yet serene and humane. The historical Buddha was now a Lord. In the northwest enormous images suggested supra-terrestrial power. In Japan, Emperor Shomu tried to establish himself as the counterpart of Vairocana through Nara Daibutsu.

Beauty was joined to magnitude, size became a symbol of status, the highest in rank were made the largest in size. Colossus does not only mean huge, extremely large, gigantic or titanic but also great, grand, spectacular, extravagant, overwhelming, awe-inspiring, imposing, and monumental: it indicates that size matters. Buddhism introduced the philosophy of grandeur in image-making. Buddhist temples by virtue of their size overwhelmed the viewer. Only the major divinities, that is, Shakyamuni, Bhaishajyaguru, Maitreya, Avalokiteshvara, Amitabha, and Vairocana/Rocana were sculpted large. At Sanjusangendo Hall in Kyoto, it is not size but the number of images that is overwhelming. Popularity of various sutras at different times led to a variety of images made on a grand scale.

In Afghanistan at Bamiyan, colossal statues were made. The admiration they espoused mingled with reverence and devotion to the transcendental power. The colossal images were 186 feet and 150 feet in height. For centuries pilgrims and merchants, monks and scholars, kings and nobles were attracted to the place. The images were carved out of a cliff. The details, folds of drapery, and other fillings were modelled from a thick layer of clay covered with a veneer of lime plaster. The final coating was given with lime. Then the statues were painted, and traces of blue paint were left at some places. Hiuen-tsang had described the images as made of metallic stone. Its pieces were cast separately and welded together later. Probably, when he had paid a visit, the images were covered with gold leaf or some other resplendent metal or were painted in metallic colour. The images were carved and wooden pegs were fixed to hold the robes for modelling the folds and then covered with a thick coat of mud mixed with chopped straw. Finally, they were plastered and then coloured. Stylistically, the images were associated with Gandhara. The drapery was voluminous.

Brocades and precious jewels were hung on the Buddhas during the ceremonial adorning in Cambodia and Thailand. The larger image was red and the smaller was moon-white. When Hiuen-tsang visited these parts, he saw the images glittering with gold and precious ornaments. A Persian poet moved by the splendour of the adorned Buddhas sang of their pure beauty. Lines written by Persian poets in the early eleventh century seem to echo Hiuen-tsang's vision of the Bamiyan Buddha, resplendent with gold according to a geographer's account of the ceremony at Balkh.

In the middle ages, the bigger statue was known as *surkh but*, the red statue and the smaller as *khink but*. A gigantic painting of the Sun in his chariot was done on the soffit of the niche.

Following page 66: A ferocious deity of the Vajradhatu Mandala. Tibetan Buddhism developed the pantheon of the religion.

Following page 67: A Bodhisattva with a diadem of five tathagatas representing Gnosis.

Many poetical evocations suggest that the poets saw Buddhist ceremonies in the great monasteries of Bamiyan. Impressed by the evocative power of the adorned Buddha and the dazzling ritual, a poet sang in Persian in the late eleventh century:

Ander harir o holle hotanand khyel,

In asparghamha hame vin mivedar ha,

Bar sa nahade afsar-o har kaf gerefte jam,

Karde por az 'aqiq o zebarjad kenarha.

Buddha wrapped in silks and robes they are

All these sweet basils and fruit-bearing trees

Having laid their crowns on their heads and taken their cups

And filled their arms with agates and emeralds.

Many such evocations can be found in Persian poetry written in territories that largely adhered to Buddhism.

Making life-size images corresponding to the measurements of donors or sponsors was in fashion in Buddhist Asia. In China stone sculptures were made to the likeness of emperors. To arrive at colossal statues measurements were raised to multiples.

Colossal statues of Buddhas were carved from the rocks in the caves of Yun-kang. Each of the five caves contains an image 13-16 metres in height in honour of one of the five emperors. Probably they are the earliest ones. Smiling faces, elongated ears, strongly chiselled noses and lips cannot fail to impress. Folds of drapery modelled in flat bands are close to Kizil in Kucha and not to the Gandharan or Khotanese (Khotan was a very famous centre of Buddhist art and learning) figures. The most spectacular is no. 20 with its colossal Buddha with thin lips, a high-bridged nose and long ears over broad shoulders. It is the representative work of the Yun-kang grottoes and has a height of 13.7 metres. A 15.5-metre tall Buddha stands in grotto no. 18. Its dignified countenance makes it a masterpiece.

Shakyamuni in grotto no. 5 of the Yun-kang is another surviving example of colossi. The 17-metre statue has a 4.5-metre foot and its toe is bigger than an average person's height. It bends slightly forward, its head and eyebrows are lowered, the facial expression is rich and gives a feeling of warmth and kindness. Lokesvararaja in China is a masterpiece at the Lung-men caves. Its height is 17.14 metres, the head alone measures over four metres, and the ears are 1.9-metre long.

First Daibutsu of Japan: The bronze statue of Shakyamuni, popularly known as Asuka Daibutsu, is the first native colossal made by the Japanese. They were impressed by the teachings of Lord Buddha who was seen as the epitome of the Six Perfections (charity, fortitude, morality, patience, meditation, and intuitive wisdom) and the eight-fold path (right beliefs, right aspirations, right speech, right conduct, right mode of livelihood, right effort, right mindedness, and right meditation). He was seen as the enlightened one who taught: the four noble truths, the doctrine of impermanence, the Twelve Chains of Causation, nirvana, spiritual insight, the doctrine of karma, and the transmigration of soul.

At this time, a book that exerted a considerable influence on the development of Buddhist art *Buddhavatansaka Mahavaipulya Sutra* was written. It was a product of

Following page 68: Shakyamuni in the *bhumisparsha mudra*, calling an impartial witness, Earth, to bear witness to his enlightenment when the demon Mara was trying to distract him.

Following page 69: White Tara holds lotus flowers in both her hands. Her serene face bestows mercy on her devotees.

~

the contributions of Indian authors over several generations. Philosophers, artists, and devotees were inspired by its grand view of totality.

Buddhas of the light cults

Amitabha, Maitreya, and Vairocana are the three Buddhas associated with the light cults. Amitabha is one of the five Tathagatas: Vairocana, Akshobhya, Ratnasambhava, Amitabha, and Amoghasiddhi. Amitabha, Tathagata of the boundless light, whose abode is Sukhavati in the west. He sits in *dhyana mudra* or holds an alms bowl and his colour is red. He figures prominently in the *Sukhvati-vyuha-sutra, Suvarna-prabhasa-sutra,* and *Amitayur-dhyana-sutra.* He is the most popular divinity in the Pure Land sect. He pledged to create his own Buddhaland which would combine all the excellent features of the various Buddha lands. Anyone who invokes the name of Amitabha with a sincere heart can achieve rebirth in his paradise. His paradise was painted by the Chinese, Japanese, Koreans, Tibetans, and Mongols in a variety of forms.

When the immeasurable light of the Buddhas shines upon the *sadhakas,* devotees, all their sins and *karmic* hindrances are nullified. The Buddha contemplates and preaches the Dharma according to the respective capabilities of the beings. As one of the five Tathagatas, Amitabha is bejewelled. His crown and jewels mark him out as a *sambhoga-kaya* in all regal splendour. His hands are shown in the *samadhi mudra.*

He is one of the popular deities in Japan, China, Nepal, and Tibet. In Nepal the highest devotions are rendered to him at the Swayambhunatha temple, as he is the Buddha of the present aeon. Beautiful offerings are bestowed on him in the western quarter of the shrine.

Belief in Jodo or Pure Land in Japan can be traced back to the early sixth century A.D. The first known reference in Japan to the *Larger Sukhavati-vyuha sutra* appears in the writings attributed to Prince Shotoku-taishi. Tenjukoku-mandara (the Land of Heavenly Longevity) was produced after the death of the prince, after a vow had been made that the soul of the prince may rest in the heaven of Amida Buddha. During the early Nara period, priests of the Kegon, Hosso, and Sanron sects used to study the Pure Land *sutras.* Monk Chiko of the Sanron sect is said to have created a Pure Land Mandala after 640 A.D. Although the sect flourished during the late Heian and Kamakura periods, the rise was not sudden but gradual. Thus during this long span of time, Bodhisattvas of the Jodo tradition were sculpted and painted over and over again.

Vairocana: Vairocana is the first of the five Transcendent Buddhas. He is the

Amitabha, the Buddha of Immeasurable Light, sitting in Dhyana Mudra. The wooden image from the Kamakura period (1185-1333) is lacquered and gilded.

Bhaishajyaguru, the Buddha of Healing, known as Yakushi Nyorai, is from the main hall of the Yakushiji monastery, Nara, Japan. Height of the bronze is 254.6 cm. Sculpted in 688, the image has seven of the past Buddhas placed on the Halo.

~

progenitor of the Five Tathagatas. He is the immeasurable luminosity that emanates into the Five Tathagatas and reminds us of the five elements of cosmology.

The Sun symbolises light, and light is knowledge. Buddha Dipankara was apotheosised as Amitabha and later as Vairocana. Vairocana also occurs as the name of a *chakravartin*, a former incarnation of Maitreya. He is also referred to as a jewel. He is the lord of the twin mandalas, Vajradhatu and Garbhadhatu. In the Vajradhatu Mandala, he is seated on a lion in the middle of a pavilion atop Mount Sumeru surrounded by the seven seas, continents, and sub-continents.

In the Garbhadhatu Mandala, he is represented as the body of principle, the *Dharmakaya,* as it exists or as it exists in the totality of phenomenal existence. He symbolises compassion, growth, and the potentiality of the world of enlightenment. Every human being has an inherent potential or seed that can be nourished in the womb of compassion to attain enlightenment.

Vairocana represents the state of universal dominion. In that form he is known as *Ekakshara Chakravartin.* He is the sovereign of sovereigns. As a sovereign he has two forms: he holds a wheel in the bowl-bearing *mudra* or performs *jnana-mushti* (fist of knowledge) or *bodhyagri mudra* (gesture of supreme knowledge). In a number of illustrated Japanese pantheons, he is portrayed with the seven jewels of a universal monarch: the wheel, wish-granting jewel, horse, elephant, queen, general, and minister. As a universal monarch his palace is equated with the residence of Indra. His abode Sumeru has terraces of various jewels.

The Vairocana at the Todaiji monastery in Nara confirms his integral association with the state. He is the image of totality. He lives in the ocean of a lotus world surrounded by one thousand petals. Japanese Emperor Shomu accepted Vairocana as the symbol of national unity. Many such images declared as National Treasures by Japan are kept in various monasteries or museums.

According to the Nepalese tradition, he is the Adi Buddha or the first of the Dhyani Buddhas. When he is placed in the sanctum of a stupa, he is the master of the whole temple. He may also be placed between Akshobhya and Ratnasambhava.

In Japan he is the highest vehicle for the union of the individual and the universal spirit. He wears a crown and some ornaments when he is seated at the centre of a mandala. His colour is white, *Akasha* (sky) is said to proceed from him as are the organs of sight and all the colours. At the centre of the Garbhadhatu Mandala is an eight-leafed lotus that represents the heart of beings. It is the solar matrix, the mysterious sanctuary where the Sun returns each night to be reborn. Four Dhyani Buddhas and four Bodhisattvas sit on the eight petals.

The Vairocana is also worshipped as the Polar Star, Dainichinyorai, painted and clothed in white, seated on a white lotus, wearing an ornate crown and in the *dhyana mudra*. In Tibetan *thangkas* he is painted as sitting cross-legged in the *mudra* of enlightenment, *bodhyagri mudra*. But as a Dhyani Buddha he wears monk's robes and his hands are in the *dharma-chakra-pravartana-mudra*.

Buddhas of healing and longevity

Bhaishajyaguru, the healing Buddha: Bhaishajyaguru, the Healing Buddha, is worshipped to ward off illnesses and disasters and grant longevity. Since illness tends to weaken the mind and causes loss of focus, treatment is vital for those who intend to achieve enlightenment. In the Pali canon, Shakyamuni Buddha is portrayed as a great healer. The healing methods are twofold: through teaching or through miraculous healing. The king of medicine is said to be the Dharma or the Buddhist teachings in their fundamental and essential form. Devotion to the Buddha took material shape in the creation of his images.

The deity is designated by a unique title, *guru*, meaning a master or teacher. The origin of the healing cult is difficult to trace. It was an important part of the proliferation of northwestern ideas and perceptions in the Indian mainland. The *Saddharma-pundarika-sutra* written in the first century B.C. is the first to refer to Bhaishajyaguru. The *sutra* of Bhaishajyaguru was translated into Chinese several times; the earliest translation was made by Shrimitra (Buddhist monk and scholar) in A.D. 317-22.

Bhaishajyaguru gained popularity along with Shakyamuni, Amitabha, and Maitreya during the T'ang period. He was widely celebrated as the Lord of the East. The Chinese composition of a *sutra* included in the Liang (name of a catalogue of that period) bibliography was known as the 'Sutra of Bhaishajyaguru of the rays of lapis lazuli' or the '*Abhisekasutra* that wipes out sins of the past and releases one from the bond of reincarnation'. Before the fifth century, Bhaishajya existed as lesser physician deities: Bhaishajyaraja and Bhaishajyasamudgata. Bhaisajya is surrounded by twelve generals in paintings and sculptures at some places. The *Bhaishajyasutra* contains names of these twelve associates identified as the Great Yaksha Generals.

In Japan, Bhaishajyaguru was the first Buddha to be worshipped by Emperor Yomei (A.D. 585-587), who took up the newly accepted faith. On being gravely ill, Yomei ordered his image to be made in the hope of his recovery. At this point of time the Japanese were novices in Buddhism. Most likely, the Koreans suggested the remedy, they sent Buddha's images and implements for ritual worship to the ailing Japanese king. The first Buddhist image produced in Japan is of Bhaishajyaguru in the Golden Hall of the Horyuji monastery.

Sculptures and paintings play an important role in Buddhist ritual worship. The symbolic meaning is conveyed through the language of symbols, colours, gestures, and attributes.

Amitayus, Buddha of longevity: Amitayus bestows long life and sets the devotee, who meditates, free from all sins. He holds a vase of ambrosia in his hands in the *dhyana mudra*. Leaves of the Ashoka tree (Saraca asoca/Saraca indica) often sprout from the vase. He wears a diadem and royal ornaments. His colour is deep red and hair is blue.

The Sun and Moon, symbols of eternity, painted on silk scrolls in 1191 are from the Kyoogokokuji monastery, Kyoto, Japan. The seed syllable for the Sun or *Aditya* is the initial letter 'a' and for *Chandra* it is 'cha' written on the top in Shittan script.

Bodhisattvas: Saviours of humanity

Bodhisattvas are saviours who voluntarily postpone their enlightenment to help human beings gain salvation. There are any number of them due to developments in Buddhist theology, the multiplication of celestial beings, and the Bodhisattva's popularity in

73

Mahayana countries. Important Mahayana treatises like *Saddharma-pundarika-sutra* and *Avatansaka-sutra* have long lists of Bodhisattvas. Manjushri, Samantabhadra, Avalokiteshvara, Mahasthamaprapta, Akashagarbha, Kshitigarbha, Maitreya, and Vajrapani are some of the Bodhisattvas that occupy a prominent place. They have been worshipped in different forms all over the Buddhist world. With time Mahayana Buddhism became a medium of advancement of civilisation, national unification and political stabilisation. In the earliest forms of Buddhist art, in *Jataka* stories, Bodhisattvas are incarnated as men or even as animals.

From the sixth century onwards, great philosophers studied, meditated, and commented upon the concept. Sculptors and painters produced a priceless treasure portraying various Bodhisattvas in a variety of iconographic forms that are worshipped to serve social and political requirements over the past centuries. They were not only worshipped as acolytes or as divinities of inferior rank; but enjoyed independent popularity. They held the power and charm of being *sui juris*; at times they even surpassed the historical Shakyamuni.

In Japan the earliest forms of Bodhisattvas are found at the Horyuji monastery. Kudara Kannon and Guze Kannon, a pair of Bodhisattvas painted on the doors, of the Tamamushi shrine, eight acolytes Bodhisattvas stand flanking the four Buddhas, painted on the walls and eight Bodhisattvas are painted in the four corners of the Golden Hall of the Horyuji monastery. They are examples of the earliest forms. The number of Bodhisattvas and their iconographic forms kept expanding along with the belief in their divine power. They were entrusted with multiplied responsibilities that gave rise to powerful forms, like the Thousand Armed Avalokiteshvara.

In the Pure Land tradition, Avalokiteshvara and Mahasthamaprapta flank Amitabha. Eight Bodhisattvas sit around him in his paradise. Twenty-five Bodhisattvas in the Raigo tradition come down as his retinue from heaven, sitting on clouds to receive the soul of the deceased.

Manjushri: Manjushri is the Lord of Learning, *Vagishvara*. He stands for *prajna*, sits on a lion, and holds a sword to cut all intellectual entanglements to reveal the light of transcendental wisdom. He is paired with another great Bodhisattva, Samantabhadra, as the chief Bodhisattvas in the *Avatansaka Sutra*. In the *Lotus Sutra*, he comes with Maitreya. In Zen monasteries in Japan, wisdom is paired with compassion and Manjushri with Samantabhadra flank Shakyamuni. Manjushri is eternally youthful. He discovers the true nature of reality by his double-edged sword of analytic discrimination that cuts across delusions.

Eleven-Headed Avalokiteshvara: Legend explains the eleven heads of Avalokiteshvara as follows: Avalokiteshvara descended into hell, converted the wicked, liberated them, and conducted them to Sukhavati, the paradise of his spiritual father Amitabha. He discovered that for every culprit converted and liberated, another instantly took his place. His head split into ten pieces from grief and despair on discovering the extent of wickedness in the world and the utter hopelessness of saving all mankind. Amitabha caused each piece to become a head and placed the heads on the body of his spiritual son Avalokiteshvara. The heads were in tiers of three, the tenth on the top and his own image above them all. Thus, Avalokiteshvara was endowed

Left:
Chunda Devi is known as Fo-mu in Japan, translated as 'Mother of Buddhas' or the 'Mother of All the Buddhas'. The seventeenth-century bronze is from Tibet.

Right:
The Thousand-armed Avalokiteshvara is from the main hall of worship of the Toshodaiji monastery, Nara period (710-784), Japan. The image is 535.7 cms in height. It is made of lacquer and gilded, but the arms are wooden.

with twenty-two eyes instead of two so that he could see all suffering and eleven brains instead of one, to concentrate on the best means of saving mankind.

Bhaishajyaguru is flanked by Bodhisattvas Suryaprabha and Chandraprabha, symbols of eternity, surrounded by twelve generals who guard the devotees through the twelve months, one by one. As devotion to Bhaishajyaguru was first embraced by an Emperor, the cult enjoyed immense popularity in early Japan. During the seventh century, a large number of devotions were held for reviving dying emperors or members of their families, to ensure longevity, to assist the dead, and to ward off calamities. Bodhisattvas in the Bhaishajyaguru mandala are: Manjughosha, Vajrapani, Avalokiteshvara, Kshitigarbha, Sarva-nivarana-vishkambhi, Akasha-garbha, Maitreya, and Samantabhadra.

The *Lotus Sutra* contains the ageless teachings of the compassionate Shakyamuni. It was a rich theme for devotees and artists because of its promise of a spiritual reward. It became the central scripture in the thirteenth century when monk Nachiren Daishonin preached it. The range of artistic expression the *Lotus Sutra* inspired is astonishing. The Bodhisattvas of the *Lotus Sutra* are Kshitigarbha, Akashagarbha, Vajrapani, Padmapani, and Samantabhadra. The acolytes of Shakyamuni are Manjushri and Samantabhadra, Brahma and Indra. Some Bodhisattvas are present at the Buddha *parinirvana* scene; ten Bodhisattvas are sculpted in the Horyuji pagoda as seeing the *mahaparinirvana* scene.

Bodhisattvas of the Vajradhatu and the Maha-karuna-garbha mandalas were brought to Japan by the great monk Kobodaishi, the founder of the Shingon sect and Dengyodaishi, founder of the Tendai sect. Tantric-oriented Buddhism was a by-product of the official bureaucratic emphasis upon the attainment of superior abilities to benefit the nation. The tradition was systematised by Kobodaishi and Dengyodaishi, giving a new direction in the Heian period. The twin mandalas comprised a vast pantheon and played a significant role in the development of the art and thought of the coming centuries.

Bodhisattvas of the Naya tradition: The *Naya Sutra* has functioned on many levels in the activities of the Shingon sect, from the political stage to the popular. Even today the daily recitation of this sutra is a regular event in the temples of the sect throughout Japan. In the mandala, there are groups of eight Bodhisattvas, four Bodhisattvas of the directions, four primary Bodhisattvas, four Bodhisattvas of offering, four inner and four outer Bodhisattvas, the Bodhisattvas of adamantine love, pride, desire, joy, flower, fragrance, dance, song, lamp and so forth.

Cult of 33 Bodhisattvas: During the Sui and T'ang dynasties in China, the concept of the thirty-three forms of Avalokiteshvara Bodhisattvas developed into a popular cult that suited the social system. The Bodhisattvas individually enjoyed popularity, serving special interests. Some of them are placed high in the Japanese Buddhist pantheon: the Bodhisattva holding a willow branch, the White-robed Avalokiteshvara Bodhisattva or Pandaravasini, the Lotus Leaf Kannon, Waterfall Viewing Bodhisattva, Fish basket Bodhisattva, Water and Moon viewing Bodhisattva, and so forth.

Independent Bodhisattvas: These do not belong to any sect or group, neither are they acolytes of a divinity. They enjoy independent popularity by fulfilling secular and religious requirements. Some of them are the Arya, Ekadasamukha, Sahasrabhuja, Horse-headed, Cintamani Cakra, Cunda Bhagavati, Amoghapasha, and the Cintamani Avalokitesvara.

Protective divinities

Protective deities are wrathful in appearance but are full of compassion. They represent divinities as frightful energies that subdue the physical and spiritual obstacles on the way to enlightenment, protect the faithful, and lead them on the path of nirvana. Their imagery incorporates the melodramatic effects of flames and sombre colours. Vidyarajas, attendants of Mahavairocana, are the kings of knowledge and lords of magic spells. They captured the imagination of monks and devotees. Acala is an emblem of a psycho-spiritual state. He symbolises steadfastness in the face of delusion and folly. Ragaraja is the power of enlightenment within the depths of human passions. Hayagriva is worshipped by military men. Vidyadharas subdue those who are difficult when it comes to enlightenment.

FACING PAGE:

A row of lions support a divine seat. Attending figures hold umbrellas and *Chowries* (ceremonial fly whisks) as symbols of royalty. The wooden panel represents a central deity wearing a seven-tiered crown merging into the sky.

The group of four guardians or the celestial kings are not known to Vedic literature. They are believed to have played an important part in the life of Shakyamuni. Collectively known as the Four Divine Guardian Kings: Dhrtarashtra, Virudhaka, Virupaksha, and Vaishravana, they are said to be present during the sermon delivered by Shakyamuni at Vaisali. Popularly they are worshipped as guardians because of the pledge they took in the presence of the Buddha to protect the nation from all sorts of calamities, sorrows, and pestilence. Their images, often with Brahma and Indra as keepers of law and protectors of the state and complete with characteristic symbolic features and colours, are associated with the four cardinal points of the compass. Inside the halls of worship they stand in the four corners. As inhabitants of the lowest *Devaloka* (abode of the gods), dwelling as guardians of the four quarters, they keep large retinues to accompany them on their travels.

The responsibility of protecting the Buddha was undertaken by the same quartet from the moment of his conception; moreover, in the *Atanatiyasutta* they appear as

Vajra-Sattva, Tibet, seventeenth century. Ten inches in height, it is known as *rdo-rje-sems-dpah*, Soul of the Thunderbolt. Holding a *Vishvavajra* in his right hand and a bell in the left; he is often said to be the Adi Buddha.

protectors of Buddha's followers. Keeping the record of their happiness in the assemblies of Devas is their responsibility while their counsellors record the virtues of men. Their world is situated halfway up the Mount or they preside over one of the slopes of Meru assisted by twenty-eight or thirty-two generals, given command over the Sun, the Moon, the stars and the Eight types of Beings (Japanese Hachibu: *gandharva, pishaca, kumbhanda, preta, naga, yaksha, rakshasa,* and *mahabhuta*). Grotesque demons crouching obligingly act as their pedestals and have a weird expression on their faces that symbolises their role in subduing wickedness. Halos are drawn to represent the guardians' divinity and crown their royalty. Large shoes and tight-fitting armours of the northwestern style are sometimes associated with their helmets and Chinese-style long-sleeve garments are under their armours.

In the Lamaist style of Tibet, they are portrayed as giants wearing elaborate antique armour with their faces displaying awe-inspiring expressions. Their identity as kings is portrayed by five-lobed crowns bearing five Dhyani Buddhas or their seed syllables. Helmets denote the martial personality.

Shotokutaishi, a Japanese scholar-statesman devoted to Buddhist philosophy, wrote commentaries on the Buddhist sutras and delivered lectures. He laboured hard to elevate the power and prestige of the imperial line and set the country on a course of centralised reforms. He is accredited as being the first Japanese Prince to vow to construct a temple for the Four Guardians if victorious, when a short civil war broke following the death of Emperor Yomei. According to the tradition, Hokoji and Shitennoji monasteries were built by Prince Shotokutaishi and Soga-no-Umako as thanksgiving for their victory over the anti-Buddhist faction. Shotoku was in his mid-teens when he made the vow. Shitennoji dedicated to the Four Divine Kings is located in the Naniwa area in Kyoto.

Suvarnaprabhasa Sutra ascribes to the worship of the Celestial Guardians. It was elevated to a prestigious position by the early seventh century in Japan and was kept in high esteem in China, especially by the T'ien T'ai priests, and translated into their languages by virtue of royal patronage. It was first expounded in the Japanese palace and various Buddhist monasteries in A.D. 680. Again in A.D. 686, one hundred priests were invited to read it. In 692 Empress Jito gave an imperial order that on account of floods the sutra should be expounded in the capital and the four home provinces. She sent its one hundred copies to various provinces to be read without fail when the Moon of the first month was in its first quarter. In A.D. 696 an imperial order was issued to expound the *sutra* and it was ordered that every year on the last day of the twelfth month, ten persons who led a pure life should be made to enter the religion. It became the most popular *sutra* during the eighth century when national peace,

A painted clay image of Shikkokngoshin or Vajradhara, a guardian. Close to 167.5 cm in height, it was sculpted in 733 from the Sangatsudo Hall of the Todaiji monastery, Nara.

protection of the nation from disaster and damage, national unity, and divine security were the prime concerns for the emperor. *Sutra* recitation was ordered as Shitenno guard the country and help devotees attain happiness and bliss. In A.D. 741 Japanese Emperor Shomu himself intended to make the *sutra's* copies in gold characters. Provincial temples built during the eighth century were called *Konkyomyo-shitenno-gokokuji*, monasteries for protection of the country by the Four Deva Kings. Twenty monks were given responsibility to expound this sutra on the eighth day of every month.

The seventh chapter of the *Suvarnaprabhasa (Caturmaharaja parivartah)* is devoted to the Four Guardians as Great Kings. The guardians promise to protect those countries, kings and families who listen to the sutra attentively and make offerings respectfully. The *Suvarnaprabhasa-sutra* was given the most important place as it guarantees all-round protection for a country.

For many centuries the *sutra* was supposed to be the most powerful expedient both for the emperor and the state. In A.D. 1281 when Kublai Khan attacked Japan with an overwhelming force, Priest Eison (A.D. 1201-1290) propagated it. The Emperor Go Uda himself copied the sixth chapter devoted to the protection of the country by the Four Divine Kings.

Pancaraksha, five goddesses of protection and longevity: The goddesses of longevity and good deeds promise thousand-fold protection. They wear crowns and ornaments like Bodhisattvas. Their fluttering scarves symbolise the vibrant spirit. Mahasahasra Pramardini, the first among them, sits on a seat, *peetha,* in meditation. The sword carried by her symbolises wisdom and erudition. The arrow is symbolic of the comprehension of sacred principles. Her *varada mudra* means bestowal of gifts and mercy, a bow in her hand symbolises female motive power and a conch in her hand is eternal and primordial sound.

The second among the five goddesses of protection is Mahamayuri, who looks angry in appearance. Her three heads symbolise knowledge of the three spheres. The third eye on her forehead indicates her ability to see beyond the mundane world. She holds a peacock feather and an arrow in her right hand as symbols of immortality and love. The third right hand is in the *varada mudra.* In her left hand, she holds a vase full of elixir, a bow, and a jewel to symbolise inestimable spiritual value and strength.

Sheetavati is the third among the five protectresses. She is calm and wears a crown and ornaments. In her upper right hand she holds a rosary, a symbol of cyclical time and eternity. A book in her upper left is a symbol of knowledge of the sacred writings. A small banner in her lower left hand symbolises Buddhism's victory over the evil forces. The fourth among the protectresses looks placid, holds a ritual chopper in her principle hands to cut the life roots of the enemy of religion, and a human skull cup filled with blood in her left hand symbolises formidable, all-consuming power and dominance over religious enemies. A battle-axe in the left hand is meant for annihilation of the enemies.

Pratisara is the fifth among the group. She has four hands and looks serene. She sits in *vama-lalitasana*, a symbol of relaxation and royal ease. She holds a sword to symbolise wisdom and erudition, a chop-tipped noose for strangling unbelievers, a wheel to symbolise the eight-fold path of self-conquest and the Wheel of Law, a trident-topped staff to symbolise dominance over the three worlds, and a *mudgara* (a mallet) in her hand that symbolises destruction of the enemies of religion.

Kalachakra, personification of time: The *Kalachakra tantra* is an important text of Vajrayana. Kalachakra is the personification of the hope the future holds and the cycle of cosmic time. It is the myth of eternal return that directs the thoughts of humankind into an inspiring future rescued from the terror of history.

In Tibetan art, Kalachakra is blue and has a gleaming red halo. Bodies of Asanga and Rudra lie trampled under his feet. He wears a tiger skin, has twelve eyes and four faces. He is endowed with three necks and six shoulders. His hands are of four colours: blue, yellow, white, and red.

Hevajra, lord of victory: Hevajra, a Tantric Buddhist deity, is associated with victory over the enemy. The *Hevajra tantra* gives the details of the rites and ceremonies performed to worship him. His symbol is a skull and his colour is blue. He often has eight heads, sixteen arms and four legs. He is often depicted dancing on a corpse. In Southeast Asia his cult was popular in the eleventh-thirteenth century. Rites were performed for material success, wealth and power, and to ensure enlightenment through identification with all the gods. In representations, eight divine figures are seated in the cups that Hevajra holds in the left hands. Eight animals and, occasionally, a monk sit in the cup in one of his right hands.

He is generally represented in the *yab-yum* attitude and the *shakti* encircles the body of *yum* by stretching her arms. Both of them wear ornaments. All the heads of Hevajra are crowned either with a skull or a Bodhisattva crown. Ornamental ribbons flow from his girdle and he wears a long garland of skulls.

The female power

Prajna-paramita, goddess of transcendental wisdom: Prajna-paramita is the deified form of Prajna-paramita-sutra given by the Buddha himself to the Nagas to enlighten mankind to gain transcendental wisdom. As an incarnation of the divine word, she carries the *sutra*. She is also looked upon as a protective energy and mother of all the Buddhas. She is white in colour. Her hands may be in the *dharma-chakra mudra*, or the right hand may carry a white lotus and the left a blue lotus that supports the sutra. She may also hold a book in her hands.

When she takes a yellow colour, she is called Pita-prajna-paramita. As she gained popularity, her forms became numerous. She may have two arms or more with a variety of hand postures and attributes. An image of Akshobhya is sometimes seen on her headdress. Her bronze images discovered from the countries of Southeast Asia indicate the popularity of her distinct forms. In a Cambodian bronze she has eleven heads and twenty-two arms. She wears a *sarong* falling to the ankles and held by an ornate belt. She is often seen with Lokeshvara as his counterpart. In Japan she became popular when the Maha-karuna-garbha-mandala came from China. There she sits with Trailokyavijaya and Yamantaka on one side and with Achala on the other side in two different forms.

Partial view of the main hall of the *Sanju-san-den-do* Hall of the Rengeo-in monastery built in the late Heian period (894-1185). It houses 1001 images of the thousand-armed Avalokiteshvara; the average height of the wooden (lacquered and gilded) images being 170 cm.

Avalokiteshvara, sitting in the centre, is the main image of the *Sanju-san-gen-do* Hall. Forty-two major arms hold various attributes, two front arms are in the *Anjali mudra* and the lower two hold a begging bowl.

Ushnisha-vijaya, goddess of supreme victory: Recitation of the *dharani* of Ushnisha-vijaya was an act of merit for the kings in China and Japan. Its earliest Sanskrit manuscript found in Japan is kept at the Horyuji monastery. It was brought to Japan to recite on the occasion of the promulgation of its first constitution. Ushnisha-vijaya was one of the popular female deities in Tibet and Mongolia. She sits in *padmadana* with both soles up. One of her three heads is yellow, one is white, and the third is black; all have a third eye. Her attributes vary from place to place, but the most common are a thunderbolt, an image of the Buddha placed on a lotus, a vase of ambrosia held in her hands in *dhyana mudra*, a lasso, a *vajra*, a bow, and an arrow. Her hair is piled up in a chignon behind the crown, the crown that bears an image of Vairocana.

Taras, adoring the feminine principle: The adoration of the feminine principle began with Goddess Tara. She took two distinct forms, later multiplied into a group of twenty-one Taras. Other goddesses also appeared in serene and ferocious forms. Green Tara was declared the *shakti* of Avalokiteshvara. Parnashabari is her follower. In Tibet and Mongolia, most divine beings are represented with their female counterparts. Angry goddesses are represented with dishevelled hair, a third eye, ornaments, and with attributes that are Tantric in nature. Dakinis are divinities of lesser rank. They may be given angry or pacific forms.

Sarasvati and Shri Mahadevi: Sarasvati and Shri Mahadevi are two goddesses who gained wide popularity in the Buddhist world. Sarasvati is the mother of speech, eloquence, and wisdom. She is the transcendent word, the power of Brahma. She enhances divine knowledge and brings victory to overcome one's spiritual shortcomings. She disperses the black clouds of ignorance and reveals the radiance of learning. Shri Mahadevi is venerated for wealth and prosperity. In Japan, a festival called *Kichijo-gekka* has been held in their honour since the eighth century.

Goddess Tara flanked by two attending divinities and topped by Buddhas is made of sandstone, eastern India, 10th century, 108 cm in height.

Shakti, personification of power: Divine beings are represented with their female counterparts, their power, *shakti*. According to the Tibetan tradition, the coupling signifies fusion of two complementary forces: father and mother. Images are invoked from the void as an aid for meditation. A devotee purifies himself and begins to concentrate, then he identifies himself with the cosmic void. Soon he can see in his heart a throne taking shape with a seed syllable being formed upon it.

Nathas in Burma: Various identities have been given to beautiful images sitting on the floor, as devout devotees in the most polite manner, wearing tight-fitting garments and a peaked crown like that of Thai dancers. Sometimes they are depicted holding lamps to light the sacred surroundings. Such images are identified as being Natha or Brahma or Indra. But they actually seemed to look like the Goddess of Lamp who has come down from heaven on wings attached to her shoulders and knees.

Narrative art: *Jataka* stories

Jatakas are the stories that give an account of the previous births of Shakyamuni Buddha. They form a great body of legends and miracles associated with the great personality. They opened vast fields of subject matter for the arts: the life stories of the Buddha's past births. The Buddha had passed from one life to another and performed a number of virtuous deeds. He had vowed to be enlightened and attain nirvana. So the previous lives are seen as a preparatory time. The Buddha remembers the knowledge accumulated during his former lives and can reveal it to fellow creatures to make them well disposed towards him. Accumulated merits raise him from the level of a human to a Great Divine or *mahapurusha*.

Shakyamuni was born in human, divine, and animal forms in accordance with the law of action, *karma*. Each new incarnation was a step forward to a higher state of being. The Buddha's past was not the absolute black night of the void. *Jatakas* form one of the nine divisions of Buddha's teachings. They are said to be five hundred in number.

These stories were the first to be carved on stupas in relief. The effort was to instil knowledge of the certainty of action *(karma)* and show the path to overcome suffering. Life was embraced in art. In a representation, Bodhisattvas, throngs of peoples and animals, musicians and ascetics, donors and others crowed around a Buddha or a Bodhisattva. The world depicted here is not just a realistic copy of nature, it is full of powerful spiritualism. The Buddha or his symbols make up the focal point of compositions. *Jatakas* at Ajanta, Tibetan *thangkas* and images at Borobudur got their theme from the *Jatakamala* of Aryashura. Later *Avadana-kalpa-lata* became another source for them.

QUEEN MAYA, THE MOTHER OF Lord Buddha, GOING IN A CHARIOT TO Lumbini, WITH SEVERAL ATTENDANTS. THE RELIEF FROM BOROBUDUR is FROM THE UPPER SERIES OF PANELS ON THE WALLS OF THE FIRST GALLERY THAT DEPICT THE LIFE STORY OF SHAKYAMUNI ACCORDING TO THE BUDDHIST TEXT, *LALITAVISTARA*.

Sudhana and Manohara are watching a dance performance, the scene engraved on a panel from the lower part of the main wall of the first gallery of Borobudur, Central Java, Indonesia. The relief is taken from a section illustrating the story of a prince who married a nymph.

Following pages 90-91:
Tibetan monks draw a sand mandala in various colours, called the rajo-mandala.

Kalachakra-mandala, a dynamic representation of the Wheel of Time, was revealed by the Buddha in the stupa of Dhanyakataka, twelve months after his enlightenment. The three enclosures of the mandala represent the spiritual, verbal, and physical planes.

Painting: Devotion with Beauty

The Buddhist text *Mahavamsha* says that artists were commanded to depict numerous scenes from the life of the Buddha. Buddhaghosha, a monk-scholar, had illustrated a story in the *Visuddhimagga,* a Buddhist text, about a group of monks who walked from cave to cave, inspecting various paintings. The Buddha also allowed monks to decorate their abodes with paintings. Usually monks proficient in painting or the residents themselves undertook the task. The monks were asked to incorporate scenes that tended to inspire them spiritually. Indeed, the Buddha admonishes monks in the *Chulavagga*, a Buddhist text, to keep their *vihara* neat and tidy.

Ajanta: Final reflection of Gupta art

In India, the great paintings at Ajanta represent the culmination of Gupta art. The origin and development of their style lies in darkness. The paintings display sophisticated techniques, representing a time when Buddhism transformed from the early philosophical and moral concepts of Hinayana, the Lesser Vehicle, to the theistic Mahayana, the Great Vehicle.

The themes for the paintings are taken from the *Jataka* stories, from the former lives of the Buddha. The painted scenes reflect moments of meditation and depict the meritorious and virtuous deeds of Shakyamuni that enabled him to attain Buddhahood. Episode after episode of the Buddha's life are arranged systematically. The assault and temptation of Mara, the miracle at Shravasti, the Buddha's invocation of the Earth are some important events. No space is left unpainted inside the caves. Many of the paintings have been damaged, but the surviving patches are enough to hint at or even study the pristine grandeur.

Cave no. 1 at Ajanta contains some of the finest examples of world painting. It illustrates the *Shibi Jataka*, which recounts a famous episode from the *Jatakas*. The other paintings are inspired by the *Mahajanaka, Shankhapala,* and *Champeyya Jataka.* The Buddha sacrificed himself in his previous

births through and by the acquisition of virtues like *dana, prajna, sila,* and *ksanti* (charity, wisdom, morality, and forbearance respectively). In the account of the *Shasha Jataka,* he was born as a hare that jumped into a fire so that his roasted body could serve as a meal for Indra. Born as a monkey in the *Mahakapi Jataka,* he formed a bridge with his body to help his retinue escape the arrows of the king of Varanasi.

In the *Dipankara Jataka,* Shakyamuni is born as a learned *brahmin.* He heard of the Buddha Dipankara's visit to Dipavati and tried hard to gather some flowers to adore him. But all the flowers of the city had already been collected for the visit on the king's orders. Fortunately, Shakyamuni could get five flowers out of the seven that a girl had secretly kept. She gave him the flowers but with the promise that the Bodhisattva would marry her. He was overjoyed and went to offer them to Dipankara who was surrounded by a crowd. He threw the flowers and they became immobilised around the head of Dipankara. Dipankara showered rain and the crowd dispersed. But the Bodhisattva spread his hair on the muddy road so that Dipankara's feet may not get soiled. Dipankara perceived the young man's spiritual perfections and predicted his future Buddhahood. This scene is also painted at Ajanta.

Countless Buddhas in various attitudes are painted on the sidewalls of the shrine and on the walls of the antechamber in cave no. 2. Large Bodhisattvas cover the back wall of the hall. In cave 16, the Buddha is preaching a congregation. The wall paintings have been darkened and effaced but one can notice several scenes: Sujata offering *payasam* (rice pudding), offerings by Trapusha and Bhallika, the two traders who met

A group of ladies painted in cave no. 1 at Ajanta, Maharashtra, India. Artistic activities at Ajanta occurred during the rule of the Vakataka and Chalukya dynasties from the fourth to the seventh centuries. The paintings represent the culmination of the art of painting in India.

A section of a palace scene from the *Vishvantara Jataka* painted on the wall of the verandah of cave no. 17 at Ajanta. The king accompanied by his retinue is walking out of the palace after being banished; his wife, Madri, follows him.

the Buddha eight weeks after his enlightenment, and the Buddha with his begging bowl and so forth.

Cave no. 17 is an example of a rich treasure trove of paintings. The walls are embellished with various *Jatakas*. One encounters the *Chhaddanta Jataka* on the wall to the left of the main entrance; the *Mahakapi Jataka* is painted over the window and the space between the windows and small doors. The Bodhisattva is born as Prince Vessantara in the *Vessantara Jataka*. The *Jataka* relates how he goes in his chariot with his son, daughter and wife, giving away his belongings one by one and enters a hermitage. Even his children and wife were given away to a Brahmin disguised as Shakra (Indra).

Manuscript paintings

Illustrating manuscripts was an old Indian fashion. Illustrated manuscripts were reportedly copied at the famous University of Nalanda. Manuscripts are also the best examples of Buddhist miniature painting. A manuscript, the *Ashta-sahasrika-prajna-paramita*, from eastern India is the earliest known illustrated manuscript. In the manuscript, the Buddha tames the Nalagiri elephant used by his cousin Devadatta to hasten his death. He sits down and preaches the Law. The manuscript is divided into seven parts. The outer and the middle sections have paintings; the rest is for the text. Another manuscript of the same text is in 188 folios on palm leaves: it is a copy made at the University of Nalanda. The eight great events of the Buddha's life occupy the

A local female deity, Temma Namgyal, who emerged in Tibet after the arrival of Padmasambhava in the eighth century.

outer space of the first and the last pairs of folios. Prajna-paramita and Manjushri, the two divinities, are painted on the first folios. The middle pair depicts four Bodhisattvas: Maitreya, Vajrapani, Chandraprabha, and Jaliniprabha. The last two folios include two Buddhas: one is teaching; the other is relaxed in conversation with two disciples. The style of the paintings shows a close connection with Burmese artists. Pala monasteries had links with the monasteries at Pagan and other Burmese cities. In still another manuscript of the same text there are graceful and elegant Bodhisattvas, mandalas of Amitabha, Maitreya, Vajrapani, Mahashri, Tara, and so forth.

Paintings in Asia: Buddhist painting in Asia is neither merely a form of art nor is it meant for the connoisseur. It represents a transcendental world. It is a combination of spirituality and of ideal beauty by painters who had scriptures in their minds and faith in their hearts. It is their faith in Buddhism, its philosophy and morality which is a source of inspiration for moral and social, political and religious values. The flourishing art of Buddhist painting spread to many countries of Asia, but was destroyed over the centuries in India.

Bamiyan in Afghanistan was the cradle of Buddhist learning and art. The niches where the colossal images stood were entirely covered with paintings. They included figures of seated Buddhas arranged in row upon row in different *mudras* with flying *apsaras, gandharvas,* and *devatas* above them. Floral creeper designs were also used for embellishment. The body forms resemble Ajanta frescoes but the style is not purely Indian. The fluttering ribbons of their headdresses are Sassanian, the foliage motifs of Bodhisattva thrones are Gandharan, the draperies and flying scarves resemble paintings at Kizil and other sites in Turkestan.

Sri Lanka, Burma, and Thailand in the southeast accepted Buddhism in its Hinayana form; in Indonesia, Central Asia, China, and Japan it flourished in its Mahayana form. Lord Buddha, his life and teachings, and the *Jataka* stories are the major themes in Hinayana painting. Hundreds of divinities, Buddhas and Bodhisattvas, goddesses and guardians, the divinities of time and space, demigods and minor deities fascinated artists in Mahayana countries. The beauty of the paradise scenes is par excellence. The donors stand in adoration on the walls of Dun-huang in China and on stone panels in Indonesia. An idealistic approach permeates all the religious art forms in Asian countries. The artists have put in the best of their talents. So the Bodhisattvas are full of dreamy beauty and the Buddhas sit elegantly and majestically.

Thailand's mastery

Thailand has preserved a rich heritage of painting in a variety of forms that is permeated by Theravada Buddhist art and thought. The Thai art of painting is remarkably beautiful. It was derived from India and Sri Lanka but by the eighteenth and nineteenth century, it so adapted to local skills, thoughts, needs, and materials that it became their own. The Thais have a basic purpose in painting: to instruct, guide, and

The title page of a sixteenth-century imperial manuscript of the Tibetan collection of mantras. On the left side of the text is Jnana-Sattva Manjushri and on the right is Yab-Yum Vajradhara, holding a *vajra* in the right and a bell in the left hand.

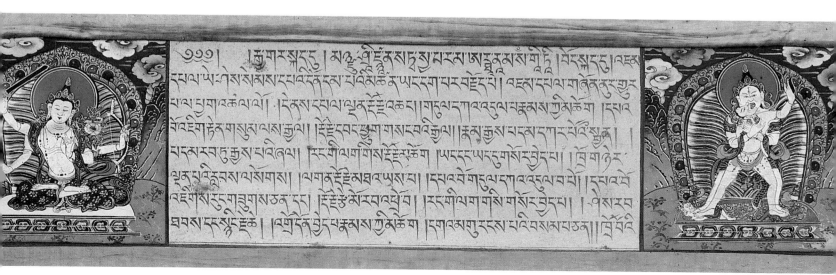

inspire the devotees through scenes taken from the *Jatakas*. Painters are often anonymous; they must have been monks or dedicated laymen.

The oldest and most important works of art are the murals on the walls of its monasteries called *wats*. Thailand had its capitals at different places during different phases of time, so Buddhist temples were built almost all over the country. Like Ajanta, the major source of themes for painting inside the walls are the *Jataka* stories. They are also meant to instruct the *bhikshus* (mendicants). The painters enlivened the walls with devotion to the law and not with a feeling of self-admiration. Unfortunately, the Thais adopted a type of dry fresco that was perishable in the humid atmosphere, which resulted in much being destroyed.

Temple complexes bear dry frescoes from shoulder-high *dados* to the dim reaches of high ceilings. Human forms in paintings look sophisticated, graceful, elegant, and beautiful. They wear tight-fitting garments, their crowns are peaked, and pointed like the *shikharas* (spires) of temples, ready to merge into the sky. The paintings look brilliant in every detail. The kingdom of Dvaravati had connections with India and Ajanta and the traditions of Sigiriya were implanted there. But only a few bits of crudely incised stones can witness the relationship today. Most probably Dvaravati paintings were similar to the works of Mons at Pagan in Burma in the twelfth century. But just traces of murals are found from Thambon Na Thom (Thailand) from the tenth to the thirteenth century. The paintings were effaced by fanatics. These murals are followed by the thirteenth-century *Jataka* scenes incised on stone slabs at Wat si chum from the Sukhothai period. They are characteristic of Thai drawing. The figures are Indianised, the style is linear, the detailed representation of jewellery is possibly taken from the Sri Lankan manuscripts brought by Thai monks.

The first fairly well-preserved paintings were from the fifteenth century (1424) from Wat Rajburana in Ayutthiya. The inner chambers of the temple have superimposed

Painting from inside the wooden cover of a sixteenth-century imperial manuscript of the Tibetan collection of mantras. Mahakala stands on a lotus and *Dpal.ldan.lha.mo* or Remati rides a horse, both are flanked by Jambhala.

rows of worshippers with a uniform background. The reliquary crypt at Wat Rajburana is equally important. Processions of Buddhas were painted in the inner chambers of Wat Mahathat built in A.D. 1374 and completed in A.D. 1388-1395. The Adoration of Buddha at Wat Sisuvannaram, Phetpuri, dated to the seventeenth century is a great mural composition.

In Thai painting, mass and line are combined and fluid. Graceful figures are first drawn with flowing contours and then filled with flat colours. Generalised landscapes fill the backgrounds, buildings, chariots, the furniture – all are set harmoniously.

Unlike western painting, Thai painting has no light and shade effect, no fixed points, no vanishing views. Time is not stopped at any particular moment, western-style perspective is not there, distance is achieved by relative placement or overlapping of figures drawn with even, flowing contours then filled with flat colours. The detailing and ornamentation are applied in a fashion similar to the Indian technique. Thai architecture is copied in the paintings: various halls are closely set with their pillars and beams and slanting roofs, shining in the bright sun and with the rich colours.

Parallel to the murals are the paintings done on cloth, mostly surviving from the eighteenth century. They are used as banners and displayed on special temple occasions. The Buddha's Great Departure, the Buddha standing with his attendants or preaching in the Deer Park, the Buddha's *parinirvana* are generally the artistic themes. Most temples also have scenes from the *Vessantara Jataka* painted on cloth, paper or wood. Such scenes are meant to inspire feelings of selfless generosity and sacrifice. The Mahajata set of paintings from Chiengmai (nineteenth century) depicts Phusati who descends from heaven to become the mother of Prince Vessantara. A majority of sets contain thirteen paintings, illustrating the many episodes of each canto.

The monks' assembly rooms are sumptuously decorated with lacquer, inlay of mother-of-pearl, gilt and glazed tiles. Gold and lacquer paintings are marvellous. Such paintings in the jewel-like structure of the Suan Pakkad palace in Bangkok display the principal events of the Buddha's life in the upper registers and scenes from the Indian epic *Ramayana* in the lower.

Characters enjoying a high status sit majestically, Buddhas are depicted in the *padmasana*, *arhats* in *ardhapadmasana*, and the laity in *vajrasana*. Guardians on window shutters and doors are unlike the fearful Chinese and Japanese figures; they are graceful and benign. Pillars inside the *wats* display items of five articles of worship, the *panchopachara*: flowers, bowls of fruits and rice, lamp, and incense.

Japanese expressions

India and Japan share a 1400-year-old cultural relationship. Buddhism reached Japan in A.D. 552 from Korea when Emperor Paekche sent gifts to the Japanese Emperor advising him to accept Buddhism as the state religion. Prior to the introduction of Buddhism into Japan by the Korean king of the Paekche dynasty, Japanese sensibilities were reflected in their pottery, clay figures, bronzes, and tomb paintings. Soon Japan turned to new and highly developed styles and techniques of art with the help of Chinese and Korean craftsmen, intellectuals, technicians, architects, sculptors, and painters. After Japanese Emperors Kimmei, Bidatsu, and Yomei, Prince Shotoku Taishi (sixth-seventh century) emerged as a fervent advocate of Buddhism.

Japanese painters shifted their energies from tombs to temples in the sixth century. Buddhism brought a revolution in Japanese life, in all the spheres of art and architecture. A highly developed and sophisticated form became dear to the hearts of the Japanese. They accepted Buddhism in the sixth century, invited artists from Korea to sculpt, to build temples, and to decorate the interiors. But they were not satisfied. Soon they began to visit China and study Buddhism and Buddhist arts.

When they received Buddhism as a religion of peace and cultural awakening, Buddhas and Bodhisattvas, *Jatakas* and paradises became dear to the Japanese. They began to paint Buddhist themes on walls, on paper, and silk. The idea behind the untiring pursuit was not merely to provide temples with interior decoration, but to create paradise on earth, to pray and perform ceremonies and to create a suitable atmosphere for the monks to meditate and to give discourses, and to discuss the philosophy of the Buddhist sutras.

Painting in Japan expresses the inner essence of what is visualised. It is the best way to express sensibilities and skills. Bright and decorative patterns under the sunshine and the foggy atmosphere that engulfed the surroundings during the rainy season gave a variety of scenes to the painters. The basic techniques and materials for Buddhist painting were brought from China. Water colours and ink on paper or silk are the most popular and fundamental methods employed in Japan. Gradually, the Japanese developed a colourful style called Yamato-e that remained their main style. The Japanese water colours are akin to tempera, they dry up quickly. The mixture of opaque white with colours produces a distinctive soft and hazy effect, different from the brilliance and transparency of oil colours.

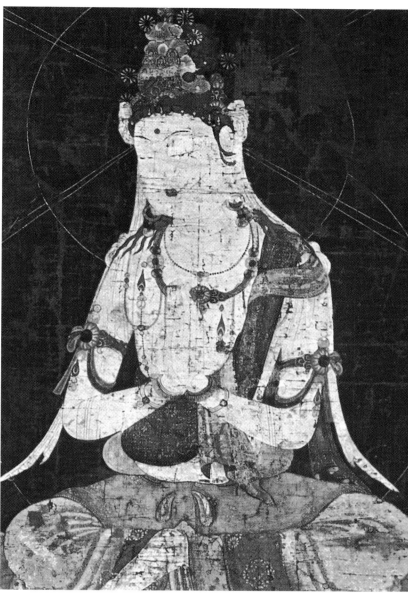

Left:

Avalokiteshvara, called Kannon
in Japan, painted on the wall
of the *Kondo* of the Horyuji
monastery built in the eighth
century near Nara.

Right:

Samantabhadra, called Fugen in
Japan, painted on a silk scroll
in the late Heian period (894-
1186); it is kept at the Tokyo
National Museum. His body is
white to symbolise purity.

Paintings on the panels, doors and back of the portable shrine, Tamamushi-no-zushi are the best and foremost examples of the Buddhist art of painting in Japan. Scenes are based on *Jataka* stories, the worshipping of Buddhist relics, and the cosmological representation of the world. The figures are full of beauty and elegance, the rocks are curved in harmony with the figures, and the empty space is filled with branches and bushes. Tamamushi-no-zushi has the oldest example of Buddhist painting but by no means can it be said to have an inferior level of artistry. Inspiration came from China through Korea but the Japanese soon became masters of techniques. The paintings are done in an abstract and sophisticated manner on a lacquer base in oil. Forms are graceful and slender, the bodies are elongated.

Murals, immortal signatures of unknown artists: The earliest murals, dated to the eighth century, are found on the walls of the major hall of worship of the Horyuji monastery set in a beautiful surrounding. These murals are reminiscent of Ajanta paintings. A Chinese monk-painter had copied most murals from Indian monasteries. Copies of his works were then transmitted to Japan, where the artists successfully tried their brush on the walls of Horyuji. Horyuji, literally, means a temple of religious prosperity (*dharma-vardhana-maha-vihara*). Inside its grand building, the paradise scenes of Amitabha, Shakyamuni, Bhaishajyaraja, and Maitreya are painted on the walls.

The Japanese had an acquaintance with, of course, the concept of paradise before the coming of Buddhism, but the visualisation of paradise with a focal point, a central divinity surrounded by Bodhisattvas, disciples, guardians, and other divine beings, came to Japan when Buddhism was transmitted from the northwestern frontiers of India. Each Buddha has his own respective paradise. Paradises are glorious abodes of peace and are the best places for souls to rest.

Buddhas and Bodhisattvas have downcast eyes, painted with a tender brush. The Bodhisattvas are full of compassion, their personalities are charming and full of noble grace. The compositions are brilliantly decorated with flying angels coming down from the heavens to occupy the upper space. Their postures have no tension, the upward fluttering of their garment gives the impression of a downward flow.

The best portion of the Horyuji murals is the western wall occupied by the paradise of Amitabha. Amitabha, the presiding deity, sits cross-legged on a lotus pedestal with his hands at chest level in the *dharma-chakra-pravartana mudra*. His chair-like throne with a back seems to be derived from West Asia. Amitabha is positioned a little higher in the frame, suggesting his position on a huge lotus with a long stem. His attendants Avalokiteshvara and Mahasthama-prapta stand on lotus flowers flanking him. Avalokiteshvara holds a vase, an image of Amitabha decorates his crown, his eyebrows are curved and eyes are downcast. The substantial quality of forms and fullness of figures shows that the art of painting had reached its zenith.

Scrolls, rolling out the divine: The painted silk scrolls exist in an extraordinary condition from the eighth century onwards. Whatever has survived from this time reflects continental influence. The portrait of the Goddess of Wealth, Lakshmi called Kichijoten in Japan, displays features of a style that had touched the heights of aesthetic beauty. It depicts idealised realism through dynamic and vital lines and colours. Large quantities of carefully prepared pigments have been applied to a piece of hemp cloth. This painting was the major object of reverence for devotional meetings.

Bodhisattva Samantabhadra, protector of the believers of the *Lotus Sutra*, sits on a six-tusked white elephant in another masterwork scroll painting from the twelfth century. White colour is used to paint the body of the Bodhisattva and the elephant to symbolise purity, a reddish tinge adds to its elegance. Shades of red, green, and blue are brilliantly used to paint the garments and the lotus seat. Application of a cut gold leaf, *kirikane,* further enhances beauty. The use of *kirikane* can be seen in a large number of scrolls. The Red-Robed Shakyamuni is an extraordinary example of this type.

Twelve hanging scrolls of Vedic deities taken into the Mahayana pantheon which are painted for the Saidaiji and Toji monasteries are the finest examples of the Late

Bottom:

Central enclosure of the
Maha-Karuna-Garbha mandala
with Vairocana sitting with
four Buddhas in the four
diretions and Bodhisattvas
in the cardinal points

Right:

The Maha-Karuna-Garbha
mandala or the Taizokai in
twelve sections is from the
Daigji monastery, Kyoto,
Japan. Monk Kobo-Daishi or
Kukai had transmitted the
mandala from China in 805.

Heian period of painting. This art is freer, effeminate, and powerful enough to create an impression of the subject's living beauty and awesomeness.

The *parinirvana* of Lord Buddha is another popular theme in Japan. Buddha entered nirvana under a tree. The leaves of the tree had withered where they had not covered him. Large-scale compositions were executed for the ceremonies celebrating nirvana. Typically, the Buddha is shown lying down to take the final rest. His disciples are in mourning, but the Bodhisattvas sit quietly witnessing the passing away of the physical body. Saints and disciples, kings and queens, priests and warriors wail and beat their breasts, angels grieve in the air, a tiger and a panther, a horse and an elephant – all are in sorrow.

Japanese painting saw a revolutionary change in the ninth century with the propagation of the Tendai and Shingon sects. The patriarchs of these sects had brought the Maha-karuna-garbha and Vajradhatu mandala*s* from China. They were painted on

The *Bija* or seed syllable 'vam' is written in the Indian script called Siddham or Shittan on a bronze plaque from Japan. 'Vam' represents Vairocana, the central divinity of the Vajradhatu-mandala.

the walls of temple interiors or on silk and hung on both sides of the altar, representing the material and the spiritual world.

The two mandalas form the core of Japanese Esoteric Buddhism and translate profound truth, including levels of meditation and the emergence of the world from the Great Source. As a psychophysical representation of the universe, the mandalas are used as a projection of the interior life in meditation, a movement from the multiple facets of existence at the lowermost level to a focused concentration at the highest point. This also leads to a realisation of the enlightenment that penetrates every sphere of existence. The Maha-karuna-garbha-mandala unfolds from its unitary centre to the diversity of its extremes in twelve sections. An important ritual and symbolic form, the mystical circle is often drawn or painted on the walls or on scrolls to be hung inside Shingon temples. The *vajrakula* or the outermost section of the Maha-karuna-garbha mandala represents the three realms: *Kamadhatu, Rupadhatu,* and *Arupadhatu.*

The seed syllables representing the deities of the central section of the Maha-Karuna-Garbha-mandala are engraved on a bronze plaque. The twin mandalas are *genzu* mandalas, often painted as a pair.

Beyond them is the world of Buddhas and Bodhisattvas in the eleven enclosures. Only by crossing these Six Levels of Existence and eight *Dhyanabhumis* is one able to concentrate on Buddhas and Bodhisattvas and, finally, on the Vairocana sitting at the centre of the mandala.

The central figure of the mandala, Mahavairocana is the Great Source and the *dharmakaya* as it exists in the totality of phenomenal existence. Mahavairocana is the source of manifestation of the infinite world and yet is inherent in each atom of existence. Being one with him is the goal of *samadhi*. Mahavairocana is the body of principle, the supreme power in Esoteric Buddhism who preaches the *dharma* in innumerable worlds in all ten directions. He is the *dharmakaya,* inseparable from *rupa* or form, and he reveals himself in formal modes in countless forms. Realisation of Mahavairocana's transcendental forms by an adherent requires the highest level of meditation. To reach that level one has to cross the Three Realms visualised in the

Maha-karuna-garbha mandala: the Realm of Desire, the Realm of *Rupa*, and the Realm of *Arupa – Kamadhatu, Rupadhatu,* and *Arupadhatu*. They represent the upward layers of the universe, the process of creation, the world in between the lowest and the highest levels of the universe.

In the Japanese painting of Shingon Buddhism, colours correspond to different stages of contemplative ecstasy, rising from black through the blue, yellow and red to white. White is a symbol of purity and is a radiant source into which all the colours have been merged and fused. These colours in different tones are prepared differently for different effects. There is black which is old, black which is fresh, lustrous black and dull black, black in sunlight and black in shadow. Other colours are mixed with black to create effects. A certain kind of rosy red is used to paint a woman's smiling face. The Japanese painters laid great stress on painting eyes as they are the most impressive and dominating feature of a face.

Raigo-zu, the descent: A new style of Buddhist painting developed with the emergence of Pure Land sects during the tenth-eleventh century. They sought an easy way of salvation – preaching devotion to Amitabha. Amitabha with his retinue of twenty-five Bodhisattvas in joyful moods is painted flying down from his heaven to receive the souls of the deceased. The style became popular as *Raigo-zu*. An attractive landscape fills the lower half of such paintings. The style makes a departure from the customary style of mandalas or mandala-based paintings.

Painting in ink: *Sumi-e* or *suiboku-ga* done in ink came to Japan in the twelfth century under the rule of the Sung and Yuan dynasties. Ink is a medium capable of creating an infinite range of shades, from the palest tones of grey to the deepest black. Skilful preparation of ink is as important as it is to fill the brush and control the pressure on its tip. Zen painters were the first to embrace this monochrome style and technique and master it to an amazing level. They portrayed the Zen philosophy, favoured by the warrior rulers, through painting. Calligraphy added greater flexibility, freedom, and power of expression.

A fundamental intuition impels Zen masters to create beautiful things. Philosophical concepts are visualised perfectly through paintings apparently looking imperfect. Landscapes are representative paintings, especially those brought from China and painted in Japan by Zen patriarchs and masters. Zen

LANDSCApE pAiNTED iN iNk iN ZEN STYLE by ThE MONk-pAiNTER SESShU, MUROMAChi pERiod (14Th-16Th cENTURY), kEpT AT ThE TOkyo NATiONAl MUSEUM. IT is A pART of AUTUMN ANd wiNTER lANdSCApES pAiNTEd follOwiNG ThE ZEN pRiNCiplES of ASYMMETRY, simpliCiTY, pURiTY, ANd TRANquiliTY.

Right:

The descent of Amitabha with six Bodhisattvas from his paradise, painted on a thirteenth-century silk scroll, Tokyo. This style of painting is called the *Raigo-zu*; it was developed by the Jodo sect. Amitabha comes down to receive the soul of the deceased.

Left:

An alcove inside the tea room of a Zen monastery with a calligraphed scroll, an *ikebana* and an art object. Sipping tea in the Zen way means cultivating the inner field of consciousness.

painting is a by-product of the purification of mind and heart. It is the finest expression of spirit that was also used as a teaching tool. The one-corner style followed by Zen monks reflects aloofness from conventional rules. They use thrifty brush painting using the least possible number of lines.

In Zen, Wabi and Sabi are two concepts that symbolise transcendental aloofness in the midst of multiplicities. Wabi means detachment from attachment, popularly translated as poverty or negativity. This leads to an innate longing for simplicity and being close to nature. There is no taste for complexities that lie on the surface of life. Beauty of imperfection accompanied by antiquity or primitive uncouthness is Sabi, loneliness. Moreover asymmetry in the Zen paintings inspires a notion of grace, solemnity, and impressiveness.

Monks in small huts are painted studying or meditating. The tiny figures look a part of Mother Nature. The painters portray grandeur and the overwhelming power of nature through their paintings. Mokuan, Mincho, Josetsu, Shubun, Sesshu, Takuan, Ikeno Taiga, Hakuin, and Suito were the master painters. In their works, the non-essential is entirely eliminated and precise details are lacking. They use the least amount of strokes. A few bold strokes result from their silent meditation. Paintings are abstract but the abstraction is not felt. They reflect physical and emotional control and spiritual concentration. Once a stroke is done, it is done forever – it is a combination of deep insight and sharp skills, a reflection of the personality of the painter.

The emptiness of space is more important than filled space. Imagination and realisation come after visualisation. Simplicity combined with elegance is non-attachment to the world of matter. Stability is derived from non-attachment. A single thing is everything.

Meditation in art: Buddha turned to himself to let meditation nourish his body and mind, one breath, one bird's song, one leaf, one ray of sunlight could serve as a subject of his meditation. He went from meditating on his body to meditate on his feelings, from feelings to meditate on his perceptions. Ultimately, he saw the oneness of his mind. A monk devotes his mind and body to realise liberation, to help himself and all others. He concentrates his efforts to help relieve suffering.

Yoga leads to exploration of consciousness from within and attainment of enlightenment. The *Bhagavad Gita* says that the first impulse to the path of yoga is sorrow. Sorrow is the first great spiritual realisation for a Buddhist also. It makes the devotee a truth-seeker, a seeker of the path of liberation, the path that leads to the extinction of suffering. It opens up the eyes of wisdom and the seeker becomes a *jnani*. And that is the end of his sorrow and the beginning of joy. Joy that belongs to the sensuous sphere is *kama-sukha* and the joy enjoyed at different levels of meditation is *dhyana-sukha*. It is self-transcending. It comes from an inner satisfaction.

A variety of mandalas were painted in China and Japan over the past 1,400 years as projections for meditation. Painter-philosophers of the Pure Land sect devoted to the worship of Amitabha produced the Taima mandala in different versions. It is based on the philosophy of *Amitayurdhyana* and *Sukhavativyuha* sutras. It offers solace from mental suffering and preaches a happy life after death in Sukhavati. The Pure Land sect devoted to the worship of Amitabha preached happiness in Sukhavati, the Paradise of Amitabha, to the faithful believers after death.

The Taima Mandala deals with the story of Ajatashatru imprisoning his parents, King Bimbisara and Queen Vaidehi; the mental suffering of the Queen, and Lord Buddha's preaching that caused her to recover from *dukha*. She listens to the teachings of Lord Buddha and begins to concentrate. She practices five *dharanas* that make her fit to practice *samadhi*. Finally, she goes into a trance and realises the bliss of Sukhavati.

Yoga is the basis of the Taima mandala. To save the people from mental suffering, to bring them to *samadhi,* it was painted several times over the past centuries and was used by Jodo sect followers for meditation. Thus, sufferings lead to concentration followed by *dharana* and *samadhi*. The story of the imprisonment of the King and the Queen by their son fills the mandala's outer left court, the sixteen meditations are in the outer right and bottom courts, and the Queen's vision of Sukhavati is in the central sanctum. The central sanctum is filled with five *dharanas*, all the architectonic elements of Sukhavati, and the paradise with Buddhas and Bodhisattvas envisioned by the Queen at various levels of *dhyana*. It was practised in Japan throughout the country from the year 760, though traces are found as early as the sixth-seventh century.

Shakyamuni preached the *Amitayurdhyana sutra* to Queen Vaidehi in Rajagriha. The *sutra* was translated and commented upon in Chinese several times; from there

A group of monks are all smiles
as they go about the rituals of
their simple yet deeply spiritual
monastic life.

it was transmitted to Japan. Queen Vaidehi listened to Shakyamuni when he outlined the ideals of a moral life. She began to cross the levels of meditation one by one. She began with the Sun in the west and went on to concentrate on the various constituents of paradise, its trees and lakes, towers, the lotus throne and so on. On completing all the sixteen stages, she suddenly had a vision of Sukhavati that fills the central sanctum.

In the centre she concentrated on the five *dharanas: parthivi, ambhasi, taijasi, vayavi,* and *akashi,* the five fundamental elements – respectively earth, water, fire, air, and sky to reach the goal. Patanjali (an Indian sage who wrote a seminal book on yoga) has said that once the mind is fixed on some point by means of *dharana,* a yogi must strive till only a single content is held in his mind. The five elements lead to bodily firmness, all the *dharanas* yield certain paranormal powers or *siddhis.*

Chinese cave art

The history of Chinese painting goes back to the time when caves were carved at Kizil in Xinjiang, China, in the second century. The murals cover an area of 4,000 square metres. The most commonly used themes are from the *Jataka* stories. Thirty-eight *Jatakas* are illustrated in Cave no. 17 in the rhomboid squares of the ceilings. The story of a monkey king saving a group of monkeys is vividly depicted in cave 69. These are the major attraction of the Thousand Buddha caves.

Dun-huang frescoes are monuments of pictorial art from the fourth to the eighth

century. *Arhats*, the immediate disciples of the Buddha, are painted rapt in intense meditation, they breathe spiritual air, they are intellectual powers. The first mention of *Arhats* in the painting dates back to the sixth century.

The subjects of Buddhist painters were endless. Varying aspects of Buddhas and Bodhisattvas were portrayed. Love and compassion found form in Avalokiteshvara; Hariti was the saviour of children. The T'ang era (618-905) stands as a period of the grandest and most perfect forms of pictorial art. A treasure of paintings comes from Dun-huang. They were permeated by Indian elements and were taken to Japan. Paintings follow Indian standards of beauty, while Chinese elements prevail in the *Jataka* theme paintings using Chinese personages, architecture, costumes, and accessories.

Chinese painting has a flow and movement of line, beauty like that of a gliding stream and is full of a sense of rhythmic motion in the floating draperies.

Shakyamuni and his two disciples in cave no. 259 of Dun-huang of the Northern Wei period. Above the niche, Maitreya sits crosslegged. Paintings based on the *sutras* adorn the side walls and present a charming combination.

The guardians of the four quarters look demonic and full of fierce energy. Avalokiteshvara in a variety of forms looks down full of compassion for humanity. There are a series of paintings of Buddhist paradise scenes. Amitabha sits majestically in his paradise, Sukhavati. The western paradise of Amitabha, eastern paradise of Bhaishajyaguru, and the paradise of Maitreya, Tushita are painted frequently. Sukhavati is represented more than a hundred times in Dun-huang and the two others more than fifty times. The story of Vimalakirti retained popularity until the end of artistic activity at Dun-huang. The figures of the donors stand below many paintings.

Stylistically and iconographically the paintings of Dun-huang are different from earlier periods. The paintings are done in tempera. The figures are heavily outlined and their feet are apart. Their faces and pointed garment folds suggest a Central Asian influence. There is a close connection between the painting and the sculpture of the caves. If the main image is rendered in relief, the subsidiary figures, the halo and the mandorla are painted on the walls behind. Painted Buddhist figures fill the available space. Some of the scenes are taken from the *sutras*.

Mural paintings in Kizil reflect the life of the people of various nationalities. Scenes of farm work present a picture of agricultural and handicraft production in Kucha around 1,400 years ago. Folk musicians are depicted in cave no 38. Kizil murals are different from Tun-huang. The images are executed in shallow colour with light and shade creating a three-dimensional effect. Sometimes the figures are outlined in iron wire lines. They are rich and varied, characterising traditional Chinese style. Flying celestial figures and musicians occupy the upper part of walls. Girls have slender figures, are dressed in tight lustrous silk, and are bare from the waist up. Some dancers pose gracefully on their toes, some musicians play *pipa* (pipe like wind instrument) while others beat drums, blow pan pipes or dance with coloured scarves.

Themes are derived from the *Jatakas* for murals painted in the caves at Kizil. Thirty-eight stories are illustrated on the wall of cave 17. Altogether there are seventy *Jatakas*, largest among all the cave murals in China. Successive scenes from the stories are painted in horizontal panels that have a common background: mountain scenery is arranged in such a way from the left to right that each part of the narrative has its space. The ceilings of the caves are decorated in an exceptionally lively manner.

A theme that has recurred innumerably in Chinese art is that of a discourse between Manjushri and Vimalakirti. Vimalakirti realises the Chinese ideals of virtue and saintliness. He holds a place of special honour in Chinese Buddhist iconography.

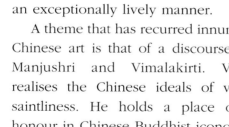

Maitreya is sitting in a niche in cave no. 251 of Dun-huang. Such icons were the focal points of devotional meditation. A treasure of art from the fifth-eighth centuries is preserved in the caves in the western Kansu area on the borders of Chinese Turkestan.

111

There is a conscious effort in the painting of the T'ang dynasty to unite calligraphy with painting. One master, Wu Tao-tzu, possessed this union of qualities to an extraordinary degree. All the people around him young or old, educated or uneducated, gathered to watch him paint the aureole of a divine being. He used to complete it with a single stroke as if a whirlwind had driven his brush. His power of imaginative realism and conception made him supreme. He painted a picture of Shakyamuni with his ten disciples. The Death of Buddha, a large composition, is a famous work he painted in A.D. 742. Here, the Buddha has entered nirvana and lies peacefully, but the monks lament the loss.

Sui-getsu-kannon or Udaka-chnadra-Avalokiteshvara sitting on the riverside under a tree, beholding the reflection of the Moon in the water. The painting decorates a ceramic plate done by a modern Chinese artist from Malaysia.

Blue, yellow, red, white, and black are colours popular in Chinese painting. Blue is associated with the east, red with the south, white with the west, black with the north, and yellow with the earth. The association of black with the north symbolises cold, likewise red indicates the fiery south. Autumn winds come from the west heralded by white frost, so white is the symbol of the west. Further, blue is associated with wood, red with fire, white with metal, black with water. These colours correspond with emotions also: white with mourning and black with worry. They correspond to emotional states of mind, too. The most glorious works were produced during the rule of the Sui and T'ang dynasties. Highly talented artists enriched the temples of the capital with wall paintings with foreign artists introducing new techniques and viewpoints. Wall paintings of the temples of the two capitals Ch'ang-an and Loyang were masterpieces made by the greatest Chinese painters. Wall paintings in the Horyuji temple in Nara were probably the last remaining works that approximate the art of the great T'ang masters. Many great artists are today represented through copies.

Hsieh Ho in the sixth century laid six canons for Chinese painting that were accepted and recognised: rhythmic vitality or spiritual rhythm expressed in the movement of life; the art of rendering the bones or anatomical structures by means of a brush; the drawing of forms which answered to natural forms; appropriate distribution of colours; composition and subordination or grouping according to the hierarchy of things; and the transmission of classic models.

Ch'an, the Buddhist meditative art: The art developed during the tenth century and stimulated the maturing of an extremely refined style of painting. Ch'an masters expressed their artistic inspiration with complete spontaneity in ink. In the splashed ink technique, contours were filled with various types of brush strokes and washes. The technique was known as Po'mo in Chinese. The beauty is that the painting does not move but suggests movement. The painting is a series of ordered relations controlled by the will to express a single idea. In Chinese art we find an instinctive avoidance of any display and a reliance on giving a subtle suggestion to the spectator's mind.

In Ch'an, landscaping is the highest sphere of art. The highest effort of art is to suggest infinity. The predominant design tries to attain a rhythmical vitality. Life is breathed into brush strokes. The finest Buddhist paintings draw the spectator out of himself and into their own ideal atmosphere to an extraordinary degree.

Chinese Ch'an painters have a different conception of design. In the paintings of Ma Yuan one meets a stimulating unexpectedness of spacing. The space for the sky is left blank above the monk. Symmetry is done away with. Imperfection has become the principle of design. The unfilled picture is left for the viewer's imagination. In some paintings, an empty space occupies the centre; a powerful instinct for largeness and simplicity prevails. A sense of utmost depth and distance is given in a small space with a few strokes. The sixteen Arhats of the Buddha was one of the favourite themes of the Cha'n painters.

Two Buddhist monks Shih-Ch'i and Shih-t'ao were popular emblematically as two stones. Shih-ch'i had entered a monastic order at a very early age and become an abbot of a monastery near Nanking. His meditating figures reflect his deep devotion to Buddhism. The art of the Sung period is known for its delicate fineness of style as contrasted to the largeness and vigour of the T'ang.

Tibet's Lamaist art

Massive lamaseries and palaces in Tibet, structures of mud, sun-dried bricks or solid stones were treasure houses of magnificent Tibetan art. The bronzes and *thangka* paintings are most popular. The great painters of Tibet used canvas and silk to paint *thangkas* that were hung inside the monasteries or carried in processions. For doing the paintings, linen or silk is stretched on a frame. Slaked lime and glue are applied on both sides. Upon drying, the surface is rubbed vigorously for a shining finish.

Lama painters keep on reciting prayers while painting. They sit on the ground, hold the canvas on the knees, and work slowly; disciples assist them. First, they draw a main vertical line at the centre to form the axis. It is identified with Mount Sumeru that stands at the centre of the universe. At the top of the axis there is a hole, the hole of Brahma, through which one leaps from self-centred existence to nirvana. Faces of Buddhas and Bodhisattvas are painted on a full moon day, and colours are applied on the new moon day. Haloes painted in graduated shades of different colours surround divine beings seated on lotus seats. Their *mudras* and attributes are full of symbolic significance.

Vegetable or mineral colours are mixed with lime and gluten. Vegetable colours were first boiled and then mixed with glue. Colours used often are lime white, red, yellow, green, vermilion, blue, and indigo. Blue and green minerals were ground from mineral rocks near Lhasa; yellow used to come from the Kham province. Red was made from mercury oxide; vermilion was imported from India. Nepal sold gold to lama painters, black was taken from the soot of pine from wood, blue from lapis lazuli, indigo from an Indian plant, and yellow from the lotus that grew near Lhasa. Lac was brought from India and Bhutan.

Gold was profusely used to paint backgrounds, ornaments, Buddhas and Bodhisattvas, and to draw rays of haloes. Minerals were ground finely; then water, glue, chalk, lacquer, and alum were mixed with them. Pine twigs were hollowed at

one side to insert goat or rabbit hair for making brushes. Split bamboo was used to draw circles.

In the tenth-eleventh century, the art of western Tibet drew inspiration from the Kashmir valley while central Tibet reflected the aesthetics of eastern India and the Pala school. The Pala-inspired central Asian style was another source for central Tibetan art.

From western Tibet, very few *thangkas* are known but illuminated manuscripts and mural paintings in Tabo and Tholing are of great value. Murals in the monasteries of Shalu Drathang and other parts of central Tibet are dated to the tenth-eleventh century.

The lustrous Newar-inspired colour scheme and the minute details of tiny scattered flowers, jewellery, and architectural elements were characteristics of the thirteenth-fourteenth century style of art. A mature Tibetan art developed out of the Pala, Kashmir, Newar, and central Asian styles during the fifteenth century. Murals at the Gyantse stupa, finished around the mid-fifteenth century, can be regarded as the starting point.

The emergence of the first major Tibetan school of painting dates back to the fifteenth century. Menla Dondrup (c. 1425-1505) founded the Menri style. It emphasises Chinese landscaping in background details. One of Dondrup's colleagues incorporated Chinese pictorial motifs in paintings that lay particular stress on the depiction of Tantric deities. Tibet witnessed a cultural renaissance in the second half of the fifteenth century

A TibetAN *thANGkA* sHows A GREAT AssEMbly of BuddHAs ANd BodHisAttvAs, sAiNts ANd pROTECTORs, RECORdiNG tHE spiRituAl HistORy of tHE pROpAGAtiON of BuddHisM iN TibET.

A *thangka* of Padmasambhava, the great teacher who went to Tibet in the eighth century, from Uddiyana in the northwest of ancient India. He was a *siddha* who had the miraculous power to conquer heathen demons. His teachings are central to the practice of the Nyingmapa sect.

Following page 116:

Shakyamuni on a 19th century Tibetan *thangka* in the *Bhumisparsha mudra* with his two disciples Shariputra and Mudgalyayana standing in front. Fourteen Buddhas are sitting around him with begging bowls in their hands.

when the Geluk order became predominant. Paintings done in the fifteenth-sixteenth century reveal delicate lines and a subtle colour scheme.

The sixteenth-seventeenth century saw several new styles emerging in central Tibet. One of them that was especially popular with the Sakya order looked towards Indian and Newar sources. It adopted the Newar style of details and its colour scheme. In another style, the figures were clad in loosely draped Chinese robes. Figures were asymmetrically organised and floating in space, in yet another style.

The second half of the sixteenth century saw the emergence of the Karma Kadri style, a style specific to east Tibet. The style developed by the artist Namkha lays emphasis on Chinese elements; blue and green landscapes are accentuated by soft shading. It became the most famous style. Haloes of *arhats, mahasiddhas,* and figures of the *Jataka* stories look translucent.

The seventeenth century saw painting flourish under the patronage of the fifth Dalai Lama. The Menri style was revived. The artists delineated a stylised realism and applied rich and thick colours. Chinese landscapes gave them a setting. Fearful protective deities were painted against the black background in the Khyenri style, which were also a favourite of the Karma Kadri style.

Tibet was politically united strongly by the fifth Dalai Lama. By virtue of this unity, regional distinctions became less prominent during the eighteenth-nineteenth century.

The Menri style was revived and was followed by artists of central and western Tibet, who produced more crowded and complex compositions. Lamas with Buddhas in paradise became a popular theme. The paintings of this period look rich as the artists applied colours thickly and treated each leaf and petal individually.

With the use of xylographs and block printing the art of making *thangkas* became stylised but unrefined. The Kham region of east Tibet maintained its own style. An incarnate Dalai Lama of the Karmapa Kagyu sect, Situ Panchen created a new style in the eighteenth century.

Mongolian style

Painting was meant for the visual understanding of Buddhist philosophy and is a major fine art in Mongolia. Fragments of mural paintings discovered during excavations bear the influence of the Uigur and Central Asian schools of painting. Murals on the walls of seven-story and five-story pagodas are found intact in some Mongol territories. Many ancient towns preserving a rich cultural heritage were deserted with the fall of the Yuan dynasty. Later the Yellow sect of Lamaism penetrated into Mongolia and achieved a strong footing in the fourteenth-fifteenth century.

Lamaism, adapted by Amdo Lama Tzong-kha-pa (1357-1419), was a branch of Mahayana Buddhism. A cultural tradition enriched by religious rites and achievements in decorative arts and architecture was introduced into Mongolia. A strong foundation was given to the monastic culture. It was once destroyed in the course of protracted wars but regained vitality again in the seventeenth century. Various branches of Buddhist culture became the core of the national artistic heritage of the Mongols.

Mongol artists have a close acquaintance with ancient Indian techniques and styles. They conformed themselves to established rules without modifications. Lama artists had written textbooks to raise artistic skills. The *Pratima-lakshana* and *Chitra-lakshana* were used as the most authoritative texts. Mongolian painters used the *dashatala* or ten-palm module and the *ashtatala*, a proportion pattern of six-eight palms, to paint major and minor gods respectively. Nine vertical, twelve horizontal, and six diagonal lines helped draw human bodies. Lines were also drawn to etch faces. Tibetan handbooks supplied the canon for depicting *Tantric* deities. All this combined together to produce exceptionally talented artists.

Buddhas and Bodhisattvas were deified human beings. They were subjects of meditation for artists who could produce images faultlessly proportionate in outward appearance. Zanabazar is one of the outstanding artists who left behind excellent examples of artistically perfect creations. He was a gifted personality in many fields of art and culture and contributed remarkably to the progress of art. He had gone to Lhasa in Tibet at the age of fifteen and was greatly honoured there. On returning, he began building temples and monasteries. As an extraordinary sculptor he cast a large number of divine images like Vajradharas, Dhyani Buddhas, twenty-one Taras, Amitayus, Buddhas, Amitabhas, Kubera, and Mahakala. His works, kept in monasteries and museums, are the finest examples of Mongolian art.

His figures embody all the thirty-two qualities and eighty signs of divine beauty. Dhyani Buddhas and Vajradharas are some of them. As a gifted artist, he has drawn admiration for many works like the Green and White Taras. The Mongol pantheon

SARASWATI, THE Goddess of Wisdom, Eloquence, and Speech, from the Aginsky Monastery, Buryatia. SHe is worshipped to disperse the black cloud of darkness. A musical instrument, *Vina*, is one of her chief characteristic features.

PRECEDING PAGE 117:
Kalachakra on a Tibetan *thangka* is represented with three eyes, four heads and thirty-two arms (drawn in four colours) holding various war-like attributes and clasping his consort. He stands in a fearful posture, trampling down two figures; the flames encircling him form a halo.

118

QUEEN MAYA GIVING BIRTH TO SIDDHARTHA. SHE STANDS IN A GARDEN IN LUMBINI, HOLDING THE BRANCH OF A TREE AND IS ASSISTED BY HER MAIDS. THE PAINTING IS FROM BURMA BY A MODERN PAINTER.

of Tantric deities is rich and varied. Dharmapalas, the guardians, look fierce. Portraits of some of the high-ranking lamas are masterpieces of portraits. The lines are amazingly refined, clear and bright shades combine to produce two-dimensional flat paintings. The use of colour is bright and shades are clear and definite in Mongol paintings.

Tibetan-like *thangkas* were made on silk or coarse cloth. The pieces were tied onto wooden boards. Milk vodka *(koumiss)* was mixed with glue and chalk dust for priming. Its surface was smoothened by the polished part of a solid metallic object and soft stone was rubbed in turns. It made the canvas smooth, thick and ready to retain the paints. Design or drawings were first transferred on a paper and then the contours of the design were punctured by a needle. Dry dye was applied along the punctured line to transfer the design to the canvas; finally, pencilling followed.

Colours were made from mineral ores. Finely ground ochre was soaked for some time in water to get a yellow dye. Nine gems were another source of acquiring paints. Ochre was burnt in a tightly covered vessel for the terracotta dye. Perfect processing produced durable paints. Brilliance was added to painting through colours made from precious stones like turquoise, lapis lazuli, coral, pearl, mother of pearl and metals such as gold, silver, copper, and iron. Gold was also used when a painting was given final touches through relief and depth and when contours were rimmed with beautiful lines. Different techniques were used to draw dynamic lines often thick in the middle and thin at both ends. When draperies or ribbons, flowers or leaves, smoke or cloud were drawn in this technique, they looked lifelike.

Some of the most outstanding examples are: Vajrapani wearing armour and garments from Turfan; an Uigur fresco image sitting with folded hands; Ratnasambhava with 108 Buddhas painted with minerals as in a *thangka* (the Buddhas are painted in white, red, blue, green, and yellow); Buddha with sixteen *Arhats*; Maitreya, the thousand-armed Avalokiteshvara with eleven heads, Ushnisha-vijaya, the Goddess of Victory holding a four-pronged *vajra*; and an image of Buddha with bow and arrow and a vase. There are also the seven-eyed White Tara, Sapta-locani; Sita Tara, Shyam Tara, and Kubera, the Lord of Wealth. The ferocious Kalachakra wears tiger's skin, tramples down demons, wear a garland of skulls, and stands in the most terrible manner. Yamantaka and Mahakala look the most ferocious. Figures are distorted to add to the macabre effect.

The depiction of Buddhist forms followed iconographic rules strictly. This showed the influence of the art of Himalayan countries (Tibet, Bhutan, Sikkim, Nepal) on Mongolian art, which had touched its zenith in the nineteenth century.

Burmese brushwork

Burmese culture flourished along the banks of the Irrawadi river originating beyond the borders of China and finally merging into the Bay of Bengal. Burma has preserved a rich heritage of painting in the form of murals, cloth paintings, and manuscript art.

The Buddhist monks of Pagan brought new forms of art and new sources for illustration. They filled the temple walls with paintings, illustrating scenes from the Buddha's life. Several thousand temples were built. Pagan became a great centre of religious and artistic activities. Frescoes and terracotta paintings from the temples of Pagan show a close affinity to the Pala art of Bengal and Bihar in style. The most interesting are the brilliantly coloured frescoes of Abeyadana. Pagan frescoes are a rich source of information about the splendour of their buildings. Countless murals based on *Jataka* stories popularised Buddhism. *Jatakas* on glazed tiles from the Ananda temple are outstanding examples. Slim bodies of flying celestials in a sinuous style are the unvarying basis for the whole later art of Burma.

Later Burmese art show a tendency towards schematic simplification. Red, yellow, green, and gold colours are slight but simple and floral decoration is simplified. Not much in the form of cloth painting has survived in Burma due to the country's climatic conditions and the fragile nature of the cloth, but some remarkable examples from Pagan still exist. Storytellers used cloth paintings, so the themes are narrative. Cloth paintings were similar to murals in style.

A thin whitish layer of gypsum and light clay was applied on the front and back of the cloth. The preliminary drawing was executed with a black pigment, paints were applied in layers, luminous colours were spread in compact fields, figures were outlined with light washes of lacquer or cinnabar, physiognomic details, folds of garments, jewellery, and leaves were finely incised with violet or black lacquer. Copper green, red ochre, vegetable lacquer, carbon black, and cinnabar were the other colours used.

Murals: The Burmese temples of the Alopi, Kubyaukgi, Ananda, and Abeyadana caves are famous for mural paintings, visualising *Jataka* stories and scenes from the life of the Buddha. The eight famous episodes from the life of the Buddha are: his birth; the Deer Park sermon; the encounter with the Nalagiri elephant; Mahaparinirvana; Descent from *Trayastrinsha* heaven; the twin miracles; the Parileyyaka episode – a monkey offering a gift of honeycomb to the Buddha; and his enlightenment.

Buddhism was brought from Thaton to Pagan. The victorious king of Pagan, Aniruddha (1044 - 1077) brought the most valuable treasures of faith, nearly the entire host of monks, and thirty-two white elephants laden with scriptures and relics. The scriptures were housed in the Bidgataik (Tripitaka library). Monks were appointed to propagate Buddhism. They were also sent to Sri Lanka for initiation into Buddhism. A Sri Lankan Buddhist order was established in Pagan.

Trayastrinsha is the second of the six Buddhist heavens and stands at the top of Mount Meru. Shakra is its king. The Buddha spent three months there to preach *Abhidhamma* to his mother. He sat in the Sudhamma meeting hall under a *parijata* tree. A ladder is leading to the earth. A shrine was erected at the spot where the Buddhas right foot touched the earth.

Manuscript art: *Parabaiks* or folding books are another fine example of Burmese painting. Paper is specially prepared and folded in a concerting fashion. It is coated with a white primer, the text is usually written in black ink above or beneath an illustration. The earliest examples of such paintings survive from the eighteenth century. Lines are drawn in black or red ink; in a later period, with a pencil. Colours are applied in a manner leading to it a flat linear appearance. They depict different scenes of Buddhist cosmology. The length of a manuscript averages ten metres. The width of a particular scene is not fixed but is normally double the opening of a book.

A number of folding books illustrate *Jataka* stories; their treatment is far more extensive than plaques or murals. More than one scene or episode is painted in a single illustration in case they require the same setting. Sometimes trees, streams, or buildings are inserted to show different parts of a narrative. The same technique is found on panels on the temple walls of Indonesia.

Lavishly decorated manuscripts are made of silk thickened by lacquer and then painted. In one such scene, Prince Siddhartha resolves to renounce his royal status, leaves his sleeping wife and baby son, and rides on his horse Kanthaka out of the palace. In another manuscript, the Buddha descends down a flight of ruby stairs flanked by gods descending via gold and silver stairs. The Buddha is preaching to his mother, assembled divinities, and spirits in heaven. His disciples are kneeling at the foot of the stairway to greet him. The Buddha is gilded, his feet rest upon a lotus as he is not walking but flying down. The umbrella upon him is a symbol of royalty.

Paintings of Anantashayana Vishnu are made in Burma and Thailand. Vishnu is shown sleeping on a huge snake called Ananta, a trifurcating lotus emerges from his navel holding Brahma, Vishnu, and Siva, the *trimurti* or trinity. Vishnu was accepted as a symbol of royalty in India and other Buddhist countries. He sustains life, and so does a king. Kings, therefore, deified themselves as Vishnu and their images in the form of Vishnu were housed in temples after their demise. The concept was emphasised during the Gupta period. Pallava royal portraits also show kings as Vishnu albeit without haloes. Paramount kings, the *Chakravartins*, were regarded as having a portion of his personality. Several stone images of Vishnu have been discovered from various sites in Thailand and Burma.

There is no perspective in Burmese painting as is the tradition of other Asian countries. But by the mid-nineteenth century Burmese painters began to use the techniques of shading, perspective, and vanishing point.

Monastic art of Sri Lanka

Buddhism was rooted in Sri Lanka with the plantation of the Bodhi Tree from Bodh Gaya during the reign of Dewanam-piya Tissa in the third century B.C. Soon it emerged as a major centre of Theravada Buddhism for South and East Asian countries. Mahavihara became the first spiritual centre of Theravada and the Abhayagiri monastery of the Mahayana in the first century B.C. Sri Lankan art flourished during two major epochs of history, Anuradhapura (third-tenth century) and Polonnaruva (eleventh-thirteenth century). The Anuradhapura school of art is closely associated with the Andhra tradition of Amaravati.

Both at Ajanta and Sigiriya, the ground was prepared by applying a basic layer of plaster of varying thickness that consisted of clay, sand, vegetable fibre, and rice husk mixed with glue. Sigirian murals are simpler than those at Ajanta. Brush strokes are rapid, bold and lively; the artists seem concerned with feminine grace and beauty. Several caves and temple buildings were painted, but today just faded figures are left. Numerous remains of paintings are reduced to patches of pigments. Some line work has been discovered from the stupas of Anuradhapura.

Sri Lankan murals executed at Sigiriya are the best examples of traces of Ajanta art. Mural paintings at Ajanta, the oldest surviving Indian paintings, embody the highest achievement of Buddhist painters. They served as models for most later works in India and other Asian countries. How the styles and technique of Ajanta travelled abroad is not an easily answered question because there are little or no available records and research work.

Green Tara, called Sgrol ljan in Tibetan, is also known as Shyama Tara. The term Tara refers to the pupil of the third eye, the eye of wisdom. The cult of Tara was propagated by Dipankara Atisha.

White Tara, called Sgrol dkar in
Tibetan, is also known as Sita
Tara or Sapta-locani Tara because
of the eyes on her palms, soles,
and forehead. Special services
are offered to her on special
days as an integral part of
the Karmapa rituals.

Further reading

1. Adrian Snodgrass, *The Symbolism of Stupa*, Cornell University, New York, 1985.
2. Benjamin Rowland, *The Ajanta Caves*, UNESCO, 1963
3. Patricia Berger and Teresa Tse Bartholomew, *Mongolia, the legacy of Chingis Khan*, Thames and Hudson, 1996.
4. Debala Mitra, *Ajanta*, Archaeological Survey of India, New Delhi, 1980 - Buddhist Monuments, Sahitya Sansad, Calcutta, 1971.
5. Elizabeth Moore, *Ancient Capitals of Thailand*, Philip Scott, Thames and Hudson, 1996.
6. Franco Ricca & Erberto Lo Bue, *The Great Stupa of Gyantse*, London, Serindia Publications, 1993.
7. Giuseppe Tucci, *Stupa: Art, Architectonics and Symbolism*, Adity Prakashan, Delhi, 1988.
8. Gorden H. Luce, *Old Burma-Early Pagan*, New York University, New York, 1969
9. Lama Aaganka Govinda, *Psychocosmic symbolism of the Buddhist Stupa*, Dharma Publishing, California 1976.
10. Laurence Binyon, *Painting in the Far East*, Dover publications Inc., New York 1959.
11. Lokesh Chandra, *Cultural Horizons of India*, Vol. 1-7, Aditya Prakashan, Delhi.
12. Lokesh Chandra, *Transcendental Art of `Tibet*, Aditya Prakashan, 1996.
13. Lusence Sickman & Alexander Soper, *The Art and Architecture of China*, Penguin Books, Australia, 1968.
14. Mary Shepherd Slusser, Nepal Mandala, *A Cultural Study of the Kathmandu Valley*, New Jersey, Princeton University Press, 1982
15. Senake Bhandaranayake, *The Rock and Wall Paintings of Sri Lanka*, Lake House Book Shop, Colombo, 1986.
16. Tsultem N, *Development of the Mongolian National Style Painting 'Mongol Zurag in Brief'*, State Publishing House, Ulaanbaatar, 1986.

Masked dancers from Tibet bring the rich colours of their festivals to the predominantly religious stance of their monastic life.

Photo Credits

Hashmat Singh:
pp. 4, 66, 67, 90-91, 114, 115, 126-127

Roli Collection:
pp. 2-3, 6, 15, 94, 95, 97, 98-99
Aditya Arya: pp. 14, 20-21, 28
Amit Pasricha: p. 23
Deepak Budhiraja: pp. 92, 96, 116, 117
Kabir Khan: pp. 50-51
Sunny Singh: pp. 19, 53 (bottom), 59 (*Courtesy:* National
Museum Collection, New Delhi)

Shashibala:
pp. 22, 24-25, 31, 35, 40, 41, 54, 55, 57, 58 (top and
bottom), 71, 73, 75 (right), 79, 82, 83, 93 (bottom),
101 (right and left), 103 (right and left),
104, 105, 106, 107 (right and left), 110,
111, 112, 119, 120, 125

Than Than Nu: p. 43

Thomas L. Kelly:
pp. 1, 7, 9, 10, 11, 16-17, 18, 21 (bottom), 27,
34, 39, 46-47, 49, 61, 94, 109, 124

Werner Forman:
pp. 12, 30, 36, 37, 52, 62, 63, 70, 75 (left),
77, 78, 84, 86-87, 88-89

Havering College Sixth Form Library

6537188

WITHDRAWN